W9-DFB-549

A

SHAKER HYMNAL

A Facsimile Edition
of the 1908 Hymnal
of the Canterbury Shakers

M
2131
.S4552
1990
seab

THE OVERLOOK PRESS
WOODSTOCK, NEW YORK 12498

First published in 1990 by
The Overlook Press
Lewis Hollow Road
Woodstock, New York 12498

Library of Congress Cataloging-in-Publication Data

A Shaker hymnal : a facsimile edition of the hymnal of the Canterbury
  Shakers / introduction by Cheryl P. Anderson.
    1 close score.
    Includes anthems.
    Reprint, with new introd. Originally published: East Canterbury,
  N.H. : Canterbury Shakers, 1908.
    1. Shakers—Hymns.   2. Hymns, English.   3. Anthems.
  M2131.S4S36   1990   90-753156
  ISBN 0-87951-402-7   CIP
                                                        M

INTRODUCTION

LOOKING AT over two hundred years of Shaker music, one can read the history of this remarkable Millennialist Christian sect. A small band of dissident Quakers from Manchester, England, led by a woman believed to be the second coming of Christ, landed in New York in 1774. Ann Lee's vision of the Kingdom of God led her and eight followers to settle on a piece of land in Niskayuna, near Albany, New York, living together in a single house, sharing their possessions and forsaking all fleshly lusts. Shaker worship in these early days had no set liturgy. The believers sat in silence and waited for the spirit of God to move one of them to say or do something. As with other Pentecostal, or charismatic, groups, Shakers were moved to speak in tongues and prophesy, move or dance "in the spirit," and sing "in the spirit." The movement "in the spirit" often took the form of a fit of trembling. It was this that mockers were ridiculing by calling the worshipers "Shaking Quakers" or "Shakers." Because the shaking was brought on by the power of God, the believers were not offended by being called Shakers and over the years have referred to themselves by that name.

In the early days, the songs that were sung in the spirit were sometimes hymns or bits of spiritual songs that originated in other Protestant traditions. Father James Whittaker, the first leader after the death of Mother Ann, often used extemporaneous original song as an extension of his preaching. Often the early songs were wordless and sung with vocables (lo del lo, etc.). The use of vocables is common in the Anglo-American folk song tradition, both in refrains of songs and as a substitute for instrumental music. The Shakers continued the folk tradition of wordless songs or sections of songs in their worship music well into the nineteenth century. Voices continued to substitute for instrumental music until the late nineteenth century, when musical instruments were finally allowed into the Shaker communities.

Although the Shaker faith originated with the teaching of Mother Ann Lee, the first official name for the sect—the United Society of Believers in Christ's Second Appearing—and the institutional form that developed later, were the creation of American converts to the faith.

iv

Father Joseph Meacham, a converted, American-born Baptist minister, was the first leader to articulate a Shaker theology. Mother Lucy Wright, a western Massachusetts native, led the sect with Father Joseph and continued as head of the church for twenty-five years after his death. Under her leadership, Shaker theology was formally worked out and written down. Perhaps the most radical beliefs of the new sect concerned the dual, male-female nature of the Godhead and the Second Coming of Christ as a female.

The new vision of God's Kingdom articulated by Mother Ann required a new form of Christian community, which didn't really begin to take form until a few years after her death in 1784. It was Father Joseph Meacham who, in 1787, began to "gather" the scattered groups of believers into communal "families," and the families into communities, and the communities into "bishoprics." As Meacham set up a system of government and organized daily life in the new communities, he felt the need for a more orderly and controlled worship form. For the first ten years of the new sect, according to elder Henry Blinn, Meacham allowed only wordless songs in worship, in order to *"wean the believers from that class of songs which they had formerly used, and which was surcharged with a mixture of theological doctrines that could not be made to harmonize with the testimony of the Cross of Christ."* These early believers replaced the spontaneous dancing in the spirit of the early worship with the "holy order" or "square order shuffle," the first formal dance that Meacham introduced for corporate worship. Consisting of Brothers and Sisters in lines on opposite sides of the meeting room, stepping forward and back three steps, the square order shuffle is more of a moving meditation than a dance. The earlier form of charismatic worship, with each person acting as the spirit moved, independently of the rest, became known as the "back" or "promiscuous" form of worship.

A religious revival in Kentucky in 1800 which facilitated the spread of Shakerism into Kentucky and Ohio also instigated a change from the wordless "solemn songs." The folk hymn that had been brought to New York and New England by the Baptists became the common music form for the revival "camp meetings" and for the new western Shaker communities. Folk hymns differ from the standard eighteenth century New England congregational singing in that the lyrics are not limited to paraphrases of the Psalms or other Scripture; rather, the text of the folk hymn is typically original devotional verse. The melody of the folk hymn, instead of being a standard Psalm tune, is a traditional or original folk tune.

The music of the revival—with a radically altered theology—became the music of the new western communities. As the new hymns came back to the eastern communities, songwriting spread throughout Shakerdom, giving voice to the newly articulated Shaker theology. Songs with words gradually supplanted the wordless solemn songs in worship. The New Lebanon leadership allowed hymns to be sung in the scheduled social gatherings of small groups of Brothers and Sisters known as union meetings in 1805, and in worship the following year. From this time on, Shaker worship services began with the singing of a hymn.

The Hancock Shaker community published the first printed Shaker hymnal in 1813. *Millennial Praises* contained 140 of the new hymns, texts only—the printing of music was an expensive undertaking and evidently beyond the capabilities of the Hancock print shop. The texts of the hymns that were chosen for *Millennial Praises* resemble the eighteenth century hymnody of Isaac Watts and the Wesleys in meter and rhyming pattern. These kinds of hymns were the familiar worship music of many of the new Shaker converts, and the borrowing was not necessarily conscious—even hymns that were received in visions follow the same forms.

Although the hymns in *Millennial Praises* served an educational purpose within the communities by expounding the new Shaker doctrines, they were a song form not particularly suited to Shaker worship. Many have ten or more verses, and the unaccompanied singing, according to observers, tended to deteriorate as the hymn wore on. The otherwise lively, spontaneous Shaker worship meetings could be weighed down by the lengthy, formal written word. The Shaker belief in continuous revelation led them to expect constant communication from God, rendering any written word instantly obsolete. Further, the hymnals were an encumbrance for dancing. For this reason, at New Lebanon, hymnals weren't carried into worship in the early days. The hymn or hymns to be sung on Sunday would be announced earlier in the week, so that the Brothers and Sisters could look them over and sing from memory in worship.

After this first hymnal, Shaker music developed in a different way, and it wasn't until 1875 that another formal hymnal was published. The early hymns constitute a sort of transitional music form for the early believers, and the texts of this early Shaker hymnody provide a window into Shaker life and spirituality in the early nineteenth century. Some of the early hymns, like "The Strait and Narrow Way," celebrate Shaker difference and separation from what they referred to as "the World." Shaker families were cloistered, self-sustaining communes. There were four "trustees" appointed to deal with all financial matters for the community and handle all dealings with "the World." The other believers in the community seldom left the confines of their dwelling, workshops, and farm. They were not free to converse with outsiders—the Millennial Laws forbade them from even shaking hands with a non-Shaker, "unless it would appear rude not to." Many of the Shaker lyrics talk about the "worldly" sacrifice that believers were making and the "heavenly" rewards that awaited.

Shaker worship on Sunday generally began with, and sometimes ended with, a hymn. The opening hymn often served as an introduction to Shaker theology for the Shakers' many "worldly" visitors to Sunday meeting. Well-to-do city folks visiting the mineral springs for the "water cure" at Lebanon Springs, New York, would take a carriage ride up the hill on Sunday morning to attend worship at the Mount Lebanon community. They came mostly to gawk at these curious people all dressed identically in strange habits, singing at the top of their lungs with no instrumental accompaniment and marching and dancing around the room. Unlike what visitors were no doubt accustomed to, the Shakers' barrel-roofed meeting house had no fixed pews and was unadorned by crosses, stained glass windows or symbols of any sort. The doctrines expounded by hymn texts like "At Shiloh was a yearly feast / where virgins met from from west to east / these virgins were a type, at least / of those that follow Jesus; / If they went forth in dances then / why should our dancing now offend / since from the filthy lusts of men / our blessed Saviour frees us?" explained some of what these visitors were seeing. The early hymns, like the hymns in this later hymnal, extol the purity of the celibate Shaker life, of the life of simplicity, humility and perfect obedience to God though obedience to the earthly leadership of the Shaker elders and eldresses and the spiritual love of Brothers and Sisters, or offer praise to the "Heavenly Father" and "Holy Mother Wisdom."

After the opening hymn and an exhortation by an elder or eldress, dancing, or "laboring" as it was called by the believers, commenced. For laboring, a group of the best singers—four or five Brothers and four or five Sisters—would stand in the center of the worshippers to accompany the dancing with unison, vocal music. By mid century, the Shakers had introduced many dances and marches into worship, and the accompanying songs usually had words.

Laboring songs, as a rule, have only one verse, which was repeated again and again for as long as the "gift" lasted, to continue the particular dance. The lyrics of these songs often use movement as a metaphor for the communal spiritual travel, as in the case of "My dear companions let's move on, the strong shall help the weak along / with joy in our hearts and a cheering song and all move on together. / We'll bear and bear, and yet forbear, and in each other's burdens share / We'll give and give and again forgive, as we would be forgiven," which was a march song.

"Extra" or "one verse standing songs" were sung by the whole congregation as a respite between dances. Even these songs often involved the whole body in worship because they were frequently sung with accompanying gestures. Gestures such as bowing and lifting the hands heavenward accentuated the meaning of lyrics such as: "To a fullness, I will serve Thee, to a fullness, O my God / For my soul this day rejoices in the power of Thy word / 'Tis refining, O I want it, let the mighty deep break up / and I will, I'll bear the washing, 'til I'm holy in Thy sight."

This early music, by Shaker law, was sung in unison and without instrumental accompaniment. Many of the songs came as inspiration, and adding harmony would be adding embellishment to something that was divinely inspired. A Shaker leader at New Lebanon said, in explanation of the Shaker ban on musical instruments, that skill on a musical instrument would breed pride in the performer. In their attitudes toward instruments, the Shakers were not too far from mainstream New England Protestants. Generally, study of music was considered frivolous, and many of the separatist churches didn't allow organs into church until the late nineteenth century.

The simplicity of the early tunes and lyrics put them well within the average believer's singing and writing skill. Because of the volume of new songs being written and the general scarcity of musical training among the converts, the Shakers needed to develop a simple way of writing down new songs so that they would be easy to save and to learn.

By the 1830s, a form of letteral notation that did not require a musical staff had been developed. Songs now could be included in correspondence between communities, and many letters from the elders of one community to the elders of another concluded with a new song. Shaker Brothers and Sisters preserved the new songs—those written by members of their community as well as songs that had been brought or sent from other communities—in handwritten song books. There are hundreds of these books extant from all of the communities, and each book is a unque collection of hymns, anthems, dance and extra songs.

The letteral notation has no symbol for a rest and no way to indicate a sharp or flat, so there are no accidentals. Songs sung in a minor key were written either in the natural or Aeolian minor that takes A as its tonic or the Dorian minor that uses D as the tonic. Many of the tunes avoid awkward intervals by using a gapped scale, like much Anglo-American folk music.

This hymnal is characteristic of a change in Shaker worship and music that began late in the nineteenth century. During the second half of the century, more apostasy and fewer converts brought the communities into numerical decline. The shrinking communities depended more and more upon the industrialized "World" for goods they were no longer manufacturing for themselves. The influence of this increased commerce with outsiders was felt in many areas of Shaker life; among them, music. A singing master friend of the believers at Canterbury convinced the family that they needed to improve their singing skills, and he started giving them music lessons in 1864. On the advice of several music teachers, the Canterbury community purchased an organ in 1870. By the 1870s other communities followed suit, and influenced by their exposure to books of gospel hymns such as those published by Moody & Sankey, Shakers began writing a new style of hymn and anthem with four singing parts. The first hymnal with conventional music notation written for keyboard accompaniment was published at Watervliet, New York, in 1875. The keyboard arrangements introduced harmony to Shaker music, and because of the restrictions of the conventional notation, together with the influence of "World's" music, Shaker music lost much of its earlier "folk" style.

Late in the nineteenth century, the average age of the believers was increasing, and fewer and fewer were able to take part in the more energetic dances. As a matter of unity, the laboring was increasingly limited to the slower, simpler dances and marching. Singing and testimonies became central to the worship service. By the twentieth century, marching was the only laboring still occasionally practiced in most of the remaining communities , so, aptly, several of the songs in this hymnal are apparently marches. Lyrics that concern travel, melodies that sound like the early laboring songs and the lack of keyboard arrangement identify songs like "There's a Light that Shines On My Pathway" (p. 239) and "Let Zion Move as the Heart of One" (p. 117) as marches.

Some of the melodies and lyrics in this hymnal recall the earlier Shaker music. The march "I Will Go On My Way" (p. 263) is perhaps the most typical of the earlier music, with its folk melody and gapped scale. As in the earlier hymns, anthems, laboring songs and extra songs, many of the texts here are expressive of Shaker theology and spirituality. Hymns like "Virgin Church" (p. 148) celebrate Shaker celibacy and consecration. The influence of the outside world can be felt, however, in the strictly scriptural text of the anthem "Give Thanks" (p. 1) or the hymn "Blessed Are the Pure" (p. 18).

Shaker music started to come full circle in the twentieth century, when young believers like Sister Mildred Barker of the Alfred, Maine, community pestered older sisters to teach them the hauntingly beautiful "old songs." Some older believers, concerned lest the early music be lost, encouraged its use in worship and singing meetings. Because of their efforts, the early music survived and has been revived. The believers today, at Sabbathday Lake, Maine, where Sister Mildred Barker went to live after Alfred closed, sing from both the later printed hymnals and from a vast repertoire of the earlier hymns, anthems, labor and extra songs that are sung from memory.

SHAKER HYMNAL

BY

THE CANTERBURY SHAKERS

"Serve the Lord with gladness: come
before his presence with singing." —
Psa. c: 2.

1908

THE CANTERBURY SHAKERS
EAST CANTERBURY, N.H.

PREFACE.

THE following repository of hymns and anthems has existed as a temporary volume for local use.

Inscribing to the memory of many authors who support their efforts from the "Other Side," the publishers at this date offer it to the public in revised form, hoping that the sentiments contained therein may serve, in a measure, to answer current inquiry, by giving expression to the Christian principles which form the bed-rock of the Shaker Church.

SHAKER HYMNAL.

Give Thanks.

"Oh give thanks unto the Lord, for he is good." — Psalm cvii : 1.

Canterbury, N. H.

O give thanks, give thanks un-to the Lord, For He is good, and His
For He is good

mer - cy en-dur-eth for ev - er. To Him which led His peo-ple thro' the
To Him which led His peo - ple

wil - der-ness, For He is good, and His mer - cy en-dur-eth for
thro' the wilder-ness, For He is good,

ev - er. He turn-ed the wil-der-ness in-to a stand-ing wa-ter,

1

and dry ground in - to wa-ter springs. Strengthen ye the weak hands and con-firm the

fee - ble knees, say to them that are of a fear-ful heart, Be strong, fear not, be -

hold your God will come, will come with a rec - om-pense. Then shall the

eyes of the blind be o - pened and the ears of the deaf, of the

deaf un - stop-ped. And a high-way shall be there, and it shall be call - ed the

way, the way of ho - li - ness, The unclean shall not pass o - ver it, the

un- clean shall not pass o - ver it, But the re-deem-ed of the Lord shall walk there-

in ; And the ran-somed of the Lord shall re - turn and come to Zi - on,

To Zi - on with songs and ev - er - last- ing joy up - on their heads, they shall ob -

tain joy and gladness, and sor - row and sigh- ing shall flee a - way.

Millennial Praise.

"Break forth into joy, sing together, ye waste places of Jerusalem."— Isaiah lii : 9.

Enfield, N. H.

Break forth in - to sing - ing, Break forth in - to sing-ing, ye vir - gin sons and

daugh-ters of the New Cre - a - tion. For now is come sal - va - tion, for

now is come sal - va-tion, the great and glo - ri-ous day of the Lord.

This day hath the God of Heav - en set up a King - dom which shall

Ad libitum.

nev- er be de-stroyed. A King- dom where-in shall dwell right-eousness and peace.

DUET.

Where the li - on and the lamb shall lie down to - geth - er, and a

lit - tle child shall lead them, and a lit - tle child shall lead them. All hail, all

hail the glo - ri - ous day. Its bright-ness is in - creas-ing, and Zi - on, fair

Zi - on is its cen - ter of light, and full-ness of power. Ma - ny shall come to

Zi - on, to Zi - on to hear and to know of the word of the

Lord. The lame who would walk, The blind who would see, the deaf and the
dumb who re - stor - ed would be, Shall come un - to Zi - on, blest
Cit - y of God, re - joice in their call - ing and promised re - ward.

Morning Herald.

"And I will rejoice in Jerusalem, and joy in my people: and the voice of weeping shall be no more heard in her, nor the voice of crying."— Isa. lxv : 19.

Canterbury, N. H.

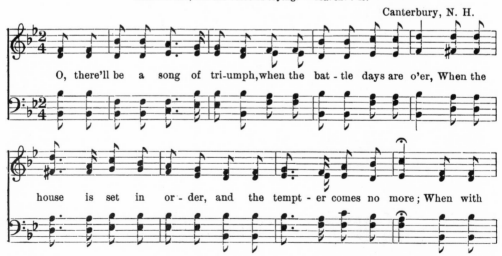

O, there'll be a song of tri - umph, when the bat - tle days are o'er, When the
house is set in or - der, and the tempt - er comes no more; When with

pur - i - ty of pur-pose thy whole life to God is given, All the world can-not con -

tain it, it will rise for joy to Heaven. It will rise, a morn-ing her-ald of Mt.

Zi - on's tra - vail here; And the hosts be - yond the lim - it of the

tem-ple and the sphere Will re - peat "as in Heav-en, up - on earth thy will is

done;" For "thy king- dom" is es - tab - lished, glo - rious vic - to-ries are won.

Exalt the Lord.

" Exalt the Lord our God, and worship at his holy hill. — Psalms xcix : 9.

Canterbury, N. H.

Ex - alt   the Lord ! Ex - alt   the Lord our God,   and wor-ship at   His ho - ly

hill.   Serve   the Lord with glad-ness and come be - fore His pres - ence   with

sing - ing. De-light thy-self   in the Lord, and He will give thee the de-sires of thine

heart.   How ex - cel - lent   is Thy lov - ing-kind-ness,   O   God !   Thy

right - eous-ness   is   like   a   great moun - tain,   Thy   judg-ments are   a

great deep. With Thee is the foun - tain of life, ... In Thy
the foun-tain of life,

light shall we see light. Cast me not a - way from Thy

pres-ence, and take not Thy ho - ly spir - it from me. Re-store un - to me the

joy of Thy sal - va - tion, and up - hold me with Thy free spir - it; For

Thou art the God of my strength, my trust and my glo - ry. I will praise Thee,

Exalt the Lord.

I will praise Thee, I will praise Thee, O . . my God, I will give
thanks un - to Thy ho - ly name, for - ev - er and for - ev - er, ev - er - more.

Fear Not.

"Fear thou not; for I am with thee: be not dismayed; for I am thy God."—Isa. xli: 10.

Canterbury, N. H.

Fear thou not, for I am with thee, I have called thee by My name.

Fear thou not, for I am with thee, I have called thee by My name.

When thou pass - est

By My name I have called thee, by My name. When thou pass - est

Our Strength.

"Praise the Lord; for the Lord is good : sing praises unto his name; for it is pleasant."— Psa. cxxxv: 3.

Canterbury, N. H.

Praise ye the Lord, O praise ye the Lord; Praise, praise the Lord for - ev - er more.

Praise ye the Lord! Praise ye the Lord! Praise ye the Lord for - ev - er more! For

He is our strength, He is our strength, He is our strength, our pres -ent help, Our

in His name we trust, For in His name we trust;

strength and present help. For in His name, For in His name we trust; For

Alto.

in His name we trust, we place our trust.

in His name, for in His name we place our trust.

For the Lord is

For the Lord is good;

For the Lord is good, the Lord is good; The

For the Lord is good, the Lord is good;

good, The Lord is good, the Lord is good;

Lord our God is good; His mer - cy, His mer - cy en - dur - eth for - ev - er.

Alto. *Slower.*

Bless - ed are they who love the Lord, who put their trust in Him.

Bass.

tempo.

Bless - ed are they, bless - ed are they, Bless - ed are they who love .. the

Lord, who put their trust, their trust in Him. For the Lord tak - eth

Duet.

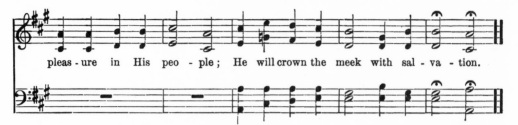

pleas - ure in His peo - ple; He will crown the meek with sal - va - tion.

Rest.

" Let Thy mercies come also unto me, O Lord, even thy salvation ; for thy judgments are good.'' — Psalm cxix : 41.

Canterbury, N. H.

Thy good - ness hath cov - ered the land, Thy mer - cies have com-passed the sea,

With joy and re - joic - ing I stand That judg - ment hath come un - to me.

Too fee - ble my powers to tell The rest that hath en - tered my soul ; En -

gage me, em - ploy as Thou wilt, I have strength if Thy spir - it con - trol.

Blessedness of Love.

"And I will refine them as silver is refined, and will try them as gold is tried."—Zech. xiii: 9.

Mt. Lebanon, N. Y.

O the bless-ed-ness of love that is pure! Tried like sil-ver in re-
fin-er's fire, Till in bright-ness of per-fec-tion and grace
Shines the like-ness of the Pu-ri-fi-er. All of dark-ness fad-eth
in its light, Sor-rows melt like morning mists a-way; Doubting ceas-es, heav-y
cares grow light, Wea-ry feet walk cheer-ful-ly the way.

16

Supplication.

"Give ear to my prayer, O God; and hide not thyself from my supplication."—Psa. lv : 1.

Enfield, N. H.

Hear us, Hear us, O righteous God, Hear us, Hear us ; Hear our sup-pli-ca-tion.

Hear us, Hear us ;

In hu-mil-i-ty we come in-to Thy house of pray'r.

Give us strength, O Lord, we pray, To re-new our lives to Thee.

O-pen Thy av-e-nues of bound-less love, Thy fountains of life-giv-ing wa-ters.

Bless us, O Lord, Bless us with Thy bless-ing.

Bless us, O Lord, Bless us,

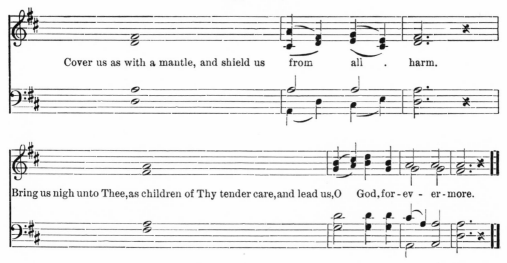

Cover us as with a mantle, and shield us from all . harm.

Bring us nigh unto Thee, as children of Thy tender care, and lead us, O God, for - ev - er - more.

My Call.

"God hath saved us, and called us with a holy calling."—2 Tim. i : 9.

Canterbury, N. H.

I'll brave the storm and breast the wave The way of God to keep; For in the har-vest

of my life Its pow - er I would reap. And when the wa - ters o - ver - flow Or

judgment take my all, God's love and mer-cy still I know, I can-not doubt my call.

Blessed are the Pure.

"Blessed are the pure in heart, for they shall see God."— Matt. v : 8.

Enfield, N. H.

Bless - ed are the pure, the pure in heart, for they shall see God. They shall

stand as sav-iours on the mount of Zi - on,—A light, bea-con light, to the

na - tions a-broad. They shall be clad in the vest-ments of pur - i - ty,

Such as the an - gels in hea - ven do wear — Sub - jects prepared for the

kingdom of glo - ry, To go no more out from its por-tals so fair.

Purest Blessing.

"Whatsoever things are lovely, whatsoever things are of good report, * * * think on these things."—
Phil. iv : 8.

Canterbury, N. H.

1. Shun the thorn and grow the flow-er, Speak no sen - ti - ment un - kind;
2. Let thy deeds like sun - light fall - ing Where the shad-ows oft - en stray,
3. Best, a - mid the pearls that glit-ter In the vic - tor's di - a - dem,

Let thy life, like balm - y show - ers, Give sweet fra - grance to the mind.
And thy voice in lov - ing ac - cents Cheer the wea - ry o'er life's way !
Is the one of pur - est wa - ter—Love—the bril - liant, spark-ling gem.

For with days so swift - ly pass - ing, Friends may go and come no more ;
We are all so prone to er - ror, Gifts of love and gos - pel care
This the ha - lo of our Sav - iour, This the glo - ry of His strife,

Let them bear thy pur - est bless - ing,—Giv - ing but re - fills thy store.
Are the sweet - est joys that min - gle With our bat - tle and our pray'r.
Let us weave its ra - diant bright - ness In the fab - ric of our life.

The Everlasting Arms.

"The eternal God is thy refuge, and underneath are the everlasting arms."— Deut. xxxiii: 27.

Canterbury, N. H.

My dis - ci - ples, for - bear ye, re - vile not a - gain, Be

low - ly of heart, said the Sav - iour of men ; And when you have con-quered the

world by the cross You'll find you have on - ly for - sak - en the dross.

Un - der - neath all the tri - als that bear you a - long Are the

Arms Ev - er - last- ing, so ten - der and strong; Then be hum-ble, be pa - tient, be

will - ing and true, For God in His mer - cy hath watch o - ver you.

The Saviour.

"He that humbleth himself shall be exalted."—Luke xiv: 11.

Canterbury, N. H.

I re-mem-ber, I re-mem - ber Those who work with me in prayer,

Who for Zi - on's sake are hum - ble, Doubt-ing nev - er God hath care.

Un - to these shall come the bless -ing, And things suf - fered now to be

Yet shall work ex - ceed - ing glo - ry, Which their souls shall feel and see.

Blessings of To=day.

"And all these blessings shall come on thee, if thou shalt hearken unto the voice of the Lord."—
Deut. xxviii : 2.

Canterbury, N. H.

1. O the bless-ings rich and ma - ny, Which are mine to share to - day!
2. E'en the path-way where I wan-dered Is il -lumed with heav'n-ly light,

All the fount-ains of God's good-ness Seem to o - pen in my way.
Show - ing where are er - ror's foot-prints, Where the steps to glo - ry's height.

Bless - ed fruits of sweet re -pent -ance, Grown while strick- en 'neath the rod!
Lead me still, O Right-eous Pow - er, Strength-en when I climb the steep,

Bless - ed les - sons of in - struc-tion Sent to lead me home to God!
Guide me thro' the dai - ly sow - ing Till e - ter - nal life I reap.

Universal Love.

"By this shall all men know that ye are my disciples, if ye have love one to another."—St. John xiii : 35.

Canterbury, N. H.

1. Blest be that u - ni - ver - sal love For which the Chris - tian aims;
2. Be lift - ed up, O vir - gin throng, With o - pen hearts em - brace
3. Its re - al sub - jects grand - ly rise Su - pe - rior in their sway

Whose source in God is found a - bove All nar - row hu - man claims.
The prin - ci - ple which pu - ri - fies And el - e - vates the race.
O'er earth - ly loves and ten - den - cies, In ac - tion, word and way.

As towers the loft - y moun - tain top A - bove the dis - tant sea, . .
The love which seeks the good of all, In ev - 'ry land and clime, . .
Then let us join this no - ble band And seek the joy, the hope, . .

So stand the mer - its of this love In its di - vin - i - ty.
Which vi - tal - iz - es, cheers, for - gives, And ren - ders life sub - lime.
The free - dom which this love will bring, Found al - ways "High-er up."

The Kingdom of God.

"Behold the kingdom of God is within you." — Luke xvii : 21.

Canterbury, N. H.

Be - hold the tab - er - na - cle of God is with men and He will dwell with

them ; They shall be His peo - ple, They shall be His peo - ple, They shall

be His peo - ple and God shall be with them and be their God, and be their God.

QUARTET.

Fear not, ... for

Fear not, lit - tle flock, Fear not, lit - tle flock, for

it is your Fa-ther's good pleas - ure to give you the king - dom, to

give you the king - dom, it is your Fa - ther's good

pleas - ure, your Fa - ther's good pleas - ure to give you the king - dom.

The king-dom of God, the king-dom of God, the king - dom of God is with -

in, is with - in you, for be - hold, for be - hold it is with -

in . . . you, be - hold the king - dom of God is with - in . . you.

The king-dom of God is right - eous - ness and peace and joy.

Humility.

"Be clothed with humility: for God resisteth the proud, and giveth grace to the humble."—1 Peter v: 5

Canterbury, N. H.

1. With - in the Vale Hu - mil - i - ty, Life's crys - tal streams a - bide, No
2. How man - y fail in growth of soul Who climb the bar - ren height, Where
3. Here in the shad - ow of God's love Is safe - ty for the soul, Here

scorch - ing sun nor parch - ing drought Can stay the liv - ing tide. By
world - ly el - e - ments con - trol And truth is lost to sight. The
naught of - fends nor in - ter - cepts The spi - rit's wise con - trol. I

earn - est pray'r and trust - ing love, With faith and works com - bined,
Chris - tian's faith will ev - er lead Where meek - ness lends her charm,
caught a glimpse in youth's bright day Of bless - ings since made known;

The hon - est seek - er af - ter light This peace - ful Vale may find.
For on - ly those who find this grace Shall win the vic - tor's palm.
To - day these are my treas - ure - store, My ev - er - last - ing home.

Persuasion.

"He that cometh to me shall never hunger; he that believeth on me shall never thirst." — St. John vi : 35.

Canterbury, N. H.

I am car - ried be - yond the vain pleas - ures of time, As the

spir - it per - sua - sive - ly cries, "O come un - to me, ye who hun - ger and

thirst, Earth hath no e - ter - nal sup - plies. I'll lead to a foun - tain which

nev - er can fail — The light and the es - sence of truth As bread and as

wa - ter shall in thee pre - vail — A glo - ri - ous im - mor - tal youth."

Counsel.

"As for me and my house, we will serve the Lord."— Josh. xxiv : 15.

Canterbury, N. H.

1. Make the Lord thy God, who shall bring thee to judg - ment And lead thee to
2. Make the Lord thy God, for His arm is not short - ened, He hear - eth pe -

righteousness, glo - ry and peace; Make the peo - ple thine who are pa - tient-ly
ti - tions, He guard - eth His own; To the plains of peace He re - stor - eth His

seek - ing The king-dom of Christ, in its truths to in - crease. For no earth - ly
peo - ple, He giv - eth His seal to the hum - ble a - lone. With vig - il of

pow'r hath wis - dom to guide thee, And kin - dred shall fail when af -
love a - bid - ing and pa - tient, He mov - eth to bless though the

flic - tions a - bound ; From *out of the depths* cry, "O Lord, we will
tem - pest en - dure, With praise and thanks-giv - ing, O Lord, in de -

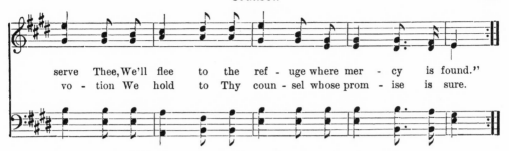

serve Thee, We'll flee to the ref - uge where mer - cy is found."
vo - tion We hold to Thy coun - sel whose prom - ise is sure.

To=day.

"Exhort one another daily, while it is called To-day."— Heb. iii: 13.

Canterbury, N. H.

No time like to-day for thine own, To-day for thy cross and thy crown;

To - day may the vic - to-ries won, Es - tab-lish thy feet in God's way.

To - day tho' the vin - tage may fail, And an - swer to prayer seem to wait, Still

let thy faith cheer thee to - day, God's bless-ings can nev - er be late.

Prayer of the Church.

"Save thy people, and bless thine inheritance: feed them also, and lift them up forever."—Psa. xxviii: 9.

Canterbury, N. H.

1. God, our Fa - ther and our Moth-er, Heed the plead-ings of our
2. Make her loy - al in Thy ser - vice Thro' in - cen-tives pure and

soul, O sus - tain, en - rich and feed us, Thro' Thy in - fi - nite con-trol.
true, Lord, re - vive Thy work in Zi - on, Clothe with strength Thy church a-new.

With Thy truth O mete the bless-ing, Give Thy Church suf - fi-cient grace
Pros - per, Lord, her sa - cred mis - sion, Let Thy glo - ry be her aim,

To a - bide the per - fect mold - ing Which shall fit each stone in place.
All her wan-d'ring sons and daugh-ters By the law of love re - claim.

Song of Praise.

" Praise is comely for the upright." — Psa. xxxiii : 1.

Hancock, Mass.   Canterbury, N. H.

1. While God in-spires my heart to sing, Or gives it life to beat,
2. God's pow'r di - vine my spir - it fills, My high - est theme in - spires;
3. The fires of truth with - in my heart Ex - tin - guished ne'er shall be;

Praise off - 'rings I will free - ly bring Be - fore the mer - cy - seat.
His pres - ence all my be - ing thrills With ar - dent, pure de - sires.
Till I from sin and death de - part, All stain - less, pure and free.

This feeds my soul with hope and faith, And love which nev - er dies;
What bless - ings hour - ly on me pour, In chas - t'ning and in love !
I will be faith - ful ev - er - more While life and strength are giv'n,

And sheds there- on a liv - ing warmth From bright ce - les - tial skies.
What mer - cies rich, an end - less store, De - scend - ing from a - bove !
That with the ran - somed I may find E - ter - nal peace and heav'n.

Infinite Love.

"Judgment also will I lay to the line, and righteousness to the plummet."— Isaiah xxviii : 17.

Canterbury, N. H.

Infinite Love.

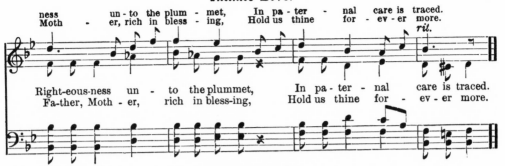

ness   un - to the plum - met,   In pa - ter - nal   care is traced.
Moth - er, rich in bless - ing,   Hold us thine   for - ev - er more.

Right-eous-ness un - to the plummet,   In pa - ter - nal   care is traced.
Fa-ther, Moth - er,   rich in bless-ing,   Hold us thine   for - ev - er more.

Draw Near.

" I have loved thee with an everlasting love ; therefore with loving-kindness have I
drawn thee."— Jer. xxxi : 3.

Canterbury, N. H.

Why fear Me when the feet may stray, Temp-ta - tion lure thee day   by day?

I   am the guide, the liv - ing way, And I would be   thy   Sav - iour.

I   know the force of hu - man ill, Yet bid   thee trust, be saved who will ; The

voice of   love will guide thee still, Re - joice, and live for - ev - er.

Trust.

"Behold, the Lord's hand is not shortened, that it cannot save." — Isa. lix : 1.

Enfield, N. H.

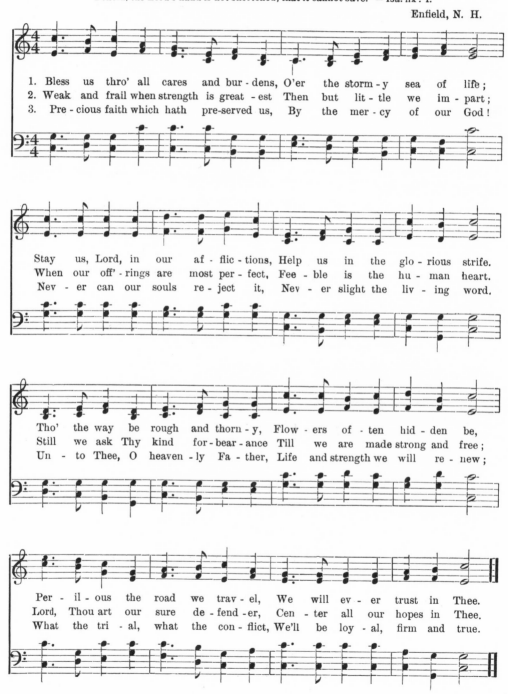

1. Bless us thro' all cares and bur - dens, O'er the storm - y sea of life;
2. Weak and frail when strength is great - est Then but lit - tle we im - part;
3. Pre - cious faith which hath pre-served us, By the mer - cy of our God!

Stay us, Lord, in our af - flic - tions, Help us in the glo - rious strife.
When our off' - rings are most per - fect, Fee - ble is the hu - man heart.
Nev - er can our souls re - ject it, Nev - er slight the liv - ing word.

Tho' the way be rough and thorn - y, Flow - ers of - ten hid - den be,
Still we ask Thy kind for - bear - ance Till we are made strong and free;
Un - to Thee, O heaven - ly Fa - ther, Life and strength we will re - new;

Per - il - ous the road we trav - el, We will ev - er trust in Thee.
Lord, Thou art our sure de - fend - er, Cen - ter all our hopes in Thee.
What the tri - al, what the con - flict, We'll be loy - al, firm and true.

God's Love.

"Nor height, nor depth, shall be able to separate us from the love of God."—Rom. viii: 39.

Mt. Lebanon, N. Y.

1. O the love of God how pre-cious! Fill-ing all im-men-si-ty; And His mer-cy, O how bound-less, Last-ing as e-ter-ni-ty.
2. By this love we're led to serve Him And to bear the chasten-ing rod; By this love we hope to tri-umph In o-be-dience to His word.
3. Gra-cious Fa-ther, we sur-ren-der Time and tal-ents, all we claim; Ask-ing to be wor-thy ev-er These to of-fer in Thy name.

Guid-ing us to per-fect heav-en, Where no e-vil can in-trude; May this love so free-ly giv-en, Fill our hearts with grat-i-tude.
Bless us with that ho-ly fer-vor, That shall quick-en us to be Sons and daugh-ters of His like-ness, By the truth made whol-ly free.
May Thy love pre-serve and hold us To a life di-vine-ly pure; Light the dark-est night, O Fa-ther, With Thy love a pass-port sure.

Abiding Care.

"Neither things present, nor things to come, nor height, nor depth, shall be able to separate us from the love of God."— Rom. viii: 39.

Canterbury, N. H.

There is al - ways a care o - ver thee, o - ver thee,

Al - ways a care o - ver thee, o - ver thee, There is al - ways a care o - ver

thee, o - ver thee, There is al - ways a care o - ver thee. o - ver thee.

No dis - tance so great, no darkness so sure, that thy tho't or foot-step is

ev - er ob - scure, So broad is the law of My love, so broad is the

law of My love, So broad is the law of My love.

Devotion.

"Every one of you hath a psalm."—1 Cor. xiv: 26.

Canterbury, N. H.

No one can sing the psalm for me, Re-ward must come from la - bor; I'll

sow for peace, thus reap in truth, God's mer - cy and His fa - vor.

"All flesh is grass," I trust not there, Yet well I love my neigh - bor With

whom I join in hon - est work And share in pure en - deav - or.

Bright Day.

"Out of Zion, the perfection of beauty, God hath shined." — Psalm 1: 2.

Canterbury, N, H.

There has come un - to thee, O thou Zi - on of God, A day of thanks-giv - ing and
prayer; With thy sons free and strong let thy daugh - ters re - joice, And
bless - ed be the heart that is pure. The heart that is pure and the
hand that is true, The feet swift to car - ry glad news, I will
gird with My strength and clothe with My love, And My pow'r in their spir-its re - new.

Faint Not.

"I looked, and, lo, a Lamb stood on the mount Zion, and with him an hundred,
forty and four thousand." — Rev. xiv: 1.

Enfield, N. H.

With the hun - dred four and for-ty thou-sand I will stand on Mount Zi - on with the
heav - en - ly Lamb, Bear-ing the seal of the true o - ver-com - er, In
sac - ri - fice ren-dering all that I am. Why fear the el - ements surging around me ?
I need not faint in the heat of the day ; There is an arm that will
sure - ly sus - tain me, —Trusting I'll toil, oh, I'll watch and I'll pray.

Christ of the Ages.

"For he is our God; and we are the people of his pasture, and the sheep of his hand."—Psa. xcv: 7.

Mt. Lebanon, N. Y.

Thou Up-lift-ing Spir-it, Thou Christ of the A-ges! Draw near to us

now, be our com-fort-ing friend. Thou hast light-ed the pathway of proph-ets and

sa-ges; In times of af-flic-tion, a help-er did send. Now, in Zi-on's great

need we ask Thy as-sist-ance; We ask it in faith, may we not ask in vain;

Give us liv-ing bread, a spir-it-ual sub-stance; Give us strength the cause of

truth to main-tain. Thine shall the hon - or and glo - ry be, While the e - ter - nal

years roll on, Thou Up-lifting Spirit! Thou Christ of the A-ges ! Hear, O hear our prayer.

Fearless.

"The Lord is the strength of my life ; of whom shall I be afraid?"— Psa. xxvii : 1.

Canterbury, N. H.

Re - joice in the strength where-with I have clothed thee, Thy house be a

song of thanks-giv - ing to My name. Ye shall not be a - fraid, though

fam - ine fill the land, Walk bold - ly by the truth, and My power shall pre - vail.

The Harvest Call.

"Thrust in thy sickle, and reap: for the time is come for thee to reap; for the harvest of the earth is ripe."— Rev. xiv: 15.

Canterbury, N. H.

1. Har - vest - ers, the grain is rip - 'ning, Are ye rea - dy for the field?
2. Har - vest - ers, the sheaves are numbered ; Bring the poor, the halt, the lame,

Ye who have the call and prom - ise, Work,—the Lord will bless the yield.
For He call - eth such to serve Him By the pow - er of His name.

Har - vest - ers, thrust in the sic - kle, See, the grain is bend - ing low,
Stay for neith - er scrip nor for - ces, Where the heart is pure and true,

Ripe it wait - eth—where the reap - ers In - to earth's broad fields to go?
One with God is life tri - umph - ant, In His strength the work pur - sue.

God's Bounty.

"He that cometh to me shall never hunger; and he that believeth on me shall never thirst."—St. John vi: 35.

Canterbury, N. H.

1. I come to be fed at Thy ta - ble, So hun-gry and thirst-y of soul, O
2. I ask, and the gift straight-way com - eth ; I seek, and the treas-ure I find; I

what hath the Spir - it in keep - ing, That will my deep yearn - ing con - trol?
knock, and the door wide is o - pened Where wis - dom and pow'r are en - shrined.

Here's bread which the cross-bear-er lov - eth, Here hon - ey and milk of the word, Re-
All hun-g'ring and thirsting here ceas - eth; I faint, and the tide sur - ges near. O

fresh thy soul, cri - eth the Spir - it, The pray'r of the hum - ble is heard.
per-fect the boun-ty e - ter - nal! No fam - ine my spir - it can fear.

True Discipleship.

"Inasmuch as ye have done it unto one of the least of these my brethren, ye have done it unto me."—
Matt. xxv : 40.

Canterbury, N. H.

In - as - much as ye have done it to the least of these, Ye have
done it un - to Me. Thus the king - dom of God shall be spread a -
broad, "As the wa - ters cov - er the sea." And "do not your alms to be
seen of men," The need - y and low - ly re - gard; Con - tin - ue the
mis - sion the Sav - iour be - gan,—His dis - ci - ples pub - lish His word.

Love to God.

"Thou shalt love the Lord thy God with all thy heart." — Matt. xxii: 37.

Canterbury, N. H.

Ye can-not serve God to ac - cept - ance The mes-sage so plain - ly I

hear, Un- less thy whole life and full in - terest, In love and de - vo -tion ap - pear.

Do all to the hon - or and glo - ry of God. Keep an

eye ev - er sin - gle and free, Thus ye shall see the

truth of My word, Christ's king - dom shall come un - to thee.

Except Thou Bless Me.

"I will not let thee go, except thou bless me." — Gen. xxxii: 26.

Canterbury, N. H.

Pass me not by, O min - is - ter of bless - ing, Give me, I
pray thee, the tri - umph I crave; I seek what the heav'ns so rich - ly are
giv - ing, The power of the con - trite, the power that will save.
Wrest - ling a - new, give me fer - vor of spir - it, Em - pow - 'ring for
du - ty and mis - sion di - vine; Faith's cov - e - nant given, more firm - ly re -

newing The pledge, O my God, to be Thine, whol-ly Thine.

Soul Questioning.

"Jesus answered him, Wilt thou lay down thy life for my sake?" — St. John xiii : 38.

Canterbury, N. H.

It comes to me in still hours As I thought-ful-ly, care-ful-ly muse, Where

un - to are giv - en the powers That God hath as-signed me to use.

Thro' faith I'm sure of His jus-tice As sow-ing, the reap-ing is mine; O

Lord, grant Thy guid-ance so ho-ly That my will be sown with Thine.

Ransomed.

" He hath sent me to heal the broken-hearted, to preach deliverance to the captives, to set at liberty them that are bruised." — Luke iv: 18.

Canterbury, N. H.

1. Turn the feet of those who wan - der In - to paths of peace to move, Bless the
2. In Thy mer - cy free the cap - tive, Clothe with strength the poor and weak, Bind with

hearts of those who fal - ter With the im - press of Thy love. Bring to Zi - on all her
power of love e - ter - nal Till Thy ho - li-ness they seek. Home-ward call Thy wand'ring

chil - dren Way - ward, sin - sick, wand'ring, poor, Now, O Lord, for their sal -
chil - dren, Lead them, hold them, God of love, Till in free - dom pure and

va - tion, Let the fount of love run o'er, Let the fount of love run o'er.
guile - less, Thy al - might - y grace they prove, Thy al - might - y grace they prove.

My Cross.

"God forbid that I should glory, save in the cross of our Lord Jesus Christ."—Gal. vi : 14.

Canterbury, N. H.

1. There are ros - es on my cross, Most beau - ti - ful to see, As I
2. Plant - ed by God's kind - ly care, E - ter - nal - ly they grow, Shed-ding

turn from all the dross, From which it mak - eth free.
forth a fra - grance rare, No flower of earth doth know.

How the buds in grace un - fold, As I near - er to it
Oh I'll clus - ter these with joy, And a psalm of praise I'll

it,
A

come! Oh, I'll more than just be - hold— I'll reach and gath - er some.
sing, For I find 'tis sweet em-ploy, To hon - or Christ my King.

Near - er to it come! I'll
psalm of praise I'll sing, I

Pearl of Great Price.

"When he had found one pearl of great price, he went and sold all that he had, and
bought it." — Matt. xiii : 46.

Enfield, N. H.

I've sought thee, I've found thee, thou pearl of great price! I val-ue thee

more than the cost of my life; Thou art dear-er, more glo-rious, more

pre-cious to me, Than gems of the earth, or pearls of the sea.

Thou cloth-est my soul and thou giv-est a crown, My heart with joy

fill-est as life I lay down, While an-gels at-tend as the

keep - ers in trust, And towers of strength in the heart of the just.

Divine Care.

"Fear thou not ; for I am with thee."— Isa. xli: 10.

Canterbury, N. H.

I will dai - ly care for thee On the land or on the

sea; Be the pas - sage fierce or fair As thy Sav - iour I am there.

There to be thy bread and wine As thou mak - est My will

thine; There to be thy staff and stay As My law thou dost o - bey.

52

My Own.

"The sheep hear his voice: and he calleth his own sheep by name, and leadeth them out."—St. John x: 3.

Canterbury, N. H.

1. I call My own and they lis-ten, The Shep-herd by the sheep is known;
2. I call My own and they fol-low, So si-lent in their trust a-lone;

No stranger's voice will they fol-low, Thro' suf-fer-ing I've made them My own.
Mur-mur-ing not tho' I lead them Where en-e-mies and dan-gers are known.

In green-est pas-tures I lead them, I lay down My life that they may live; The
O righteous Shepherd, en-fold us, Con-tin-ue to lead on Thy flock; Thro'

hand of the foe can-not find them, For pro-tec-tion in the fold I give.
val-ley, o'er moun-tain, we fol-low In the shad-ow of the E-ter-nal Rock.

Troubled Waters.

"Whosoever then first after the troubling of the waters stepped in was made whole."— St. John v : 4.

Canterbury, N. H.

1. When the an - gel trou-bles the wa- ters, O then en - ter in with de - light To
2. Be-neath trou-bled wa - ters the deep-est, The soul finds God's mercy and love ; In

find a full cleans-ing of spir - it, . The tri - umph of truth and of right.
safe - ty are an-chored the pur - est, . At one with the Fa -ther a - bove.

Some doubt-ing and help-less stand wait- ing For oth- ers their ef-forts to guide, The
Then fear not the waves dashing o'er thee, Tho' tempest and storm take thine all ; Re -

brave en-ter in with re - joic - ing, Seek life in the pure Jor-dan tide.
freshed, rise in faith from its heal - ing, Re - newed to thy spir - it -ual call.

Reflection.

"No man, having put his hand to the plough, and looking back, is fit for the kingdom of God."— Luke ix : 62.

Canterbury, N. H.

1. O where should I look for the bless - ing of Heaven, If
2. Then up to the hills from whence com - eth my help I

false to the light I've re - ceived? Though an an - gel de - clare it, I've
look for my cross and my crown ; The as - sur - ance is with me that

no more as - sur - ance My soul liv - ing truth has be -
an - gels will aid me, As life to my call I lay

lieved. Then O, pre - cious guar - dians on earth and in heaven, In -
down. The strength of the heavens will . be my pro - tec - tion, The

spire me with zeal to be true,— Be true in the morn - ing, at
power of the ho - ly I claim ; My guide and my com - pass, my

noon - tide and e - ven, And each day my pur - pose re - new.
hon - est de - vo - tion, Are cen - tered in tri - umph to reign.

Law and Christ.

"Thou shalt love the Lord thy God with all thine heart."— Moses.
"Love your enemies, do good to them which hate you."— Christ.

Canterbury, N. H.

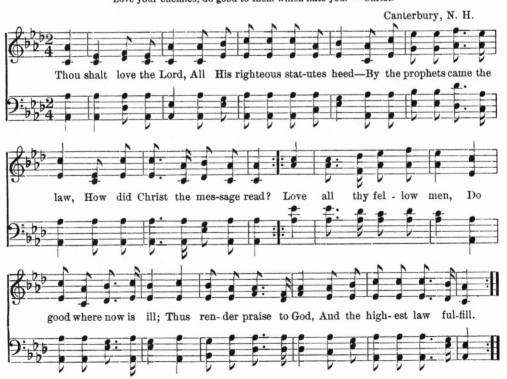

Thou shalt love the Lord, All His righteous stat-utes heed—By the prophets came the

law, How did Christ the mes-sage read? Love all thy fel - low men, Do

good where now is ill; Thus ren- der praise to God, And the high- est law ful-fill.

Prayer Universal.

"For my house shall be called an house of prayer for all people." — Isa. lvi: 7.

Canterbury, N. H.

1. The Spir - it is call - ing, ear - nest - ly call - ing, O Zi - on un -
2. O Spir - it most ho - ly, ear - nest - ly call - ing, So ten - der - ly

fold in deep prayer; O pray for the fa - thers, the sis - ters, and
plead - ing for all, In prayer - ful de - vo - tion we bow at Thy

broth - ers, O pray for the whole house-hold, O pray for the
bid - ding, To ask Thy rich mer - cies may fall Till house - hold and

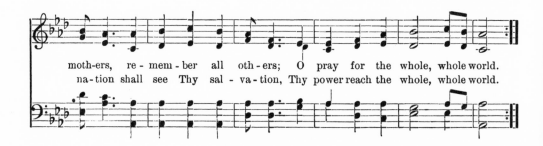

moth-ers, re - mem - ber all oth-ers; O pray for the whole, whole world.
na - tion shall see Thy sal - va - tion, Thy power reach the whole, whole world.

Anchorage with Christ.

"Kept by the power of God." — 1 Peter 1: 5.

Canterbury, N. H.

1. My lit-tle barque is frail at best, Yet trust-ing-ly I'll brave life's storm, Since
2. Have faith in God 'mid tem-pest gales, Thy an-chor-age with Christ hold fast; Who

in God's lov-ing care I rest Be-yond all fear of earth-ly harm.
trust-eth in His strength pre-vails When winds and storms of earth have passed.

With Christ as Pi-lot, ev-er near, My barque in safe-ty He will guide; As-
Now safe with-in the har-bor moored, All dan-gers calm-ly dis-ap-pear, While

sur-ance comes with words of cheer, Which ech-o far a-cross the tide.
peace and joy in sweet ac-cord To God as-cend in praise and pray'r.

Summer Land.

"Ye shall pass over Jordan to go in to possess the land which the Lord your God giveth you."—
Deut. xi : 31.

Alfred, Me.

Sweet Sum-mer Land, O land of bright glo - ry ! Thy beau - ti - ful fields are

spread out be - fore me, Thy ver - dant groves and thy vine-yards fair, And my

soul ex - claims, How won-der-ful they are, How won-der-ful they are !

Won - der-ful ! won - der-ful ! beau - ti - ful and glo - ri - ous Un - to the

soul who has come off vic - to - ri - ous O - ver the world of sin and

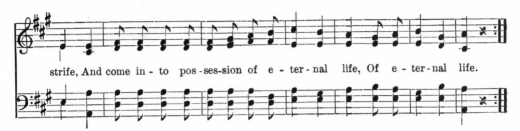

strife, And come in-to pos-ses-sion of e-ter-nal life, Of e-ter-nal life.

Remembrance.

"Not one of them is forgotten before God."—Luke xii: 6.

Mt. Lebanon, N. Y.

Not one spar-row is for-got-ten, E'en the ra-ven God will feed;

And the li-ly of the val-ley From His boun-ty hath its need.

Then shall I not trust Thee, Fa-ther, In Thy mer-cy have a share?

And through faith and prayer, my Moth-er, Mer-it Thy pro-tect-ing care?

Pledge.

"I will trust and not be afraid: for the Lord Jehovah is my strength and my song." — Isa. xii: 2.

Canterbury, N. H.

1. Shall mountains fall and val - leys rise, And roll - ing streams be still Ere I can
2. Though conflict deep my heart as - sails As du - ty's line I trace, My pur - pose

trust my Fa - ther's way And on - ly choose His will? In truth I
true, en - rich - es me With hum - ble Chris - tian grace. Re - signed, I

cheer-ful - ly re - new My pledge through prayer drawn, To keep my sac - ri -
ask no bet - ter part Than thus by faith I claim; Since Christ I serve, what

fice in view, Thy will, no more my own, Thy will, no more my own.
need I fear? I tri - umph in His name, I tri - umph in His name.

Higher Life.

"For judgment I am come into this world, that they which see not might see." — St. John ix: 39.

Canterbury, N. H.

1. O - pen to my vis - ion clear - ly   What the high - er life re -
2. Who would know the heights of glo - ry,   And the crown of life would

quires; To its truth, its love and beau - ty, My whole heart and soul as -
share, Must as - cend by walk - ing low - ly, Both the cross and bur - den

pires. For my light must be in - creas - ing, Life to me af - fords no pause;
bear. As the Pat - tern, so the prac - tice, "Fol - low me" the world for - sake,

On - ward, up - ward, nev - er ceas - ing, Are re - demp - tion's per - fect laws.
Thus the high - er life is o - pen, "Who - so - ev - er will" par - take.

Peace.

"Peace I leave with you, my peace I give unto you."—St. John xiv: 27.

Canterbury, N. H.

Peace I leave with you, My peace . I give un-to you; Not as the world

giv-eth, give I un-to you. Peace I leave with you, My peace I give

un-to you, Not as the world giv-eth, give I un-to you. Let not your

heart . . . .   neith-er let

let not your heart be trou-bled, neith-er let . . . it be a-

let not your heart   neith-er let

fraid. Let not your heart be trou-bled, Neith-er let it be a-fraid.

In My Fa-ther's house are ma - ny man - sions, In My Fa-ther's house are ma- ny

man - sions, In My Fa - ther's house are ma - ny man - sions. If it

were not so, if it were not so I would have told you, I would have

told . you. I go to pre - pare a place for you, I

go to pre-pare a place for you, . that where I am there ye may be al - so, that

where I am, there ye may be al - so, there ye may be al - so.

Peace I leave with you, My peace I give un - to you; Not as the world

giv - eth give I un - to you. Peace I leave with you, My

peace I give un - to you, Not as the world giv - eth, give I un - to

you. My peace I leave with you, My peace I give un - to you.

Redemption's Song.

"And they sing the song of Moses * * and of the Lamb." — Rev. xv: 3.

Canterbury, N. H.

1. Re - demp -tion's song, for thee I long, Thy bliss my soul would
2. I'll learn one meas - ure day by day Through stu - dy, pains and
3. This pas - sage of the vic - tor's song O let my heart re -

know, From whose rapt chords and liv - ing words Pure in - spi - ra - tions
care; And no false note, no si - ren lay, Shall plant a dis - cord
peat, In un - ion with the saint - ed throng Dis - course its mu - sic

flow; Whose notes of joy, from tri - umphs won, The vic - tors on - ly
there. I'll set it to the Gold - en Rule The Sav - iour gave; said
sweet. This is the song for which I long, The bliss my soul would

sing, And from whose voi - ces blent in one The grand - est pe - ans ring.
He — "Do un - to oth - ers as ye would That they should do to thee."
know; Its thrill - ing chords and liv - ing words From high - est sour - ces flow.

Song Eternal.

"And they sung as it were a new song ; and no man could learn that song but the hundred and forty and four thousand, which were redeemed from the earth."—Rev. xiv: 3.

Canterbury, N. H.

1. I walk a-bove thy sins, vain world,Their force shall not con-trol; Thy
2. I sing a sweet-er psalm,O earth,Than fi-nite pow'rs can sing; A-

joys, the fair-est and the best, Ne'er sat-is-fy the soul. But
bove thy dis-cord, pain and strife, I hear Heav'n's mu-sic ring— The

from the source of spir-it life The rich-est gifts de-scend, I catch the breeze and
bless-ed joy of sins forgiv'n,The peace God's angels send; I swell the song that

join the song, The song which hath no end, The song which hath no end.
rings in Heav'n,The song which hath no end, The song which hath no end.

Feed My Lambs.

"Lovest thou me more than these ? * * * Feed my lambs."— St. John xxi: 15.

Canterbury, N. H.

1. "Feed My lambs," the Spir - it cri - eth, Lest thro' hun - ger they may
2. "Feed My lambs;" tho' faint and help - less In green pas - tures gen - tly

stray, Guard them where the dan - ger li - eth Till the truth they will o - bey.
lead; Where they stray, as sav - iour fol - low, Thine to an - swer ev - 'ry need.

Truth—the Fa - ther's lov - ing pres - ence, Light, His love, His pow'r di -
Through the wil - der - ness, the val - ley, Mount, or mead, be ev - er

vine, Feed and chas - ten with this bless - ing, Till they in His like - ness shine.
there;"Feed My sheep," the Sav - iour cri - eth, This the test thy love must bear.

Excellent Way.

"And yet shew I unto you a more excellent way."—1 Cor. xii: 31.

Canterbury, N. H.

1. Have ye found a more ex - cel - lent way? Come tell of its peace and its
2. We have found the more ex - cel - lent way, Can tell of its peace and its

joy. I would share in its bless - ing to - day, My heart would its
joy; For we live in its bless - ing to - day, Its wis - dom di -

wis - dom em - ploy. I would rise in - to new - ness of life, would rise in - to
rects our em - ploy. As we rise in - to new - ness of life, we rise in - to

new - ness of life, thro' birth of the spir - it made free, And em -
new - ness of life, the spir - it of Christ mak - eth free; And the

brac - ing true spir - it - ual light, the Kingdom of Heav - en would see.
King - dom of Heav - en with - in, thro' glo - rious vict-'ries we see.

The Saviour's Promise.

"But when thou makest a feast, call the poor, the maimed, the lame, the blind."— Luke xiv : 13.

Canterbury, N. H.

I will gath - er un - to Me, saith the Sav - iour of men, The poor and de -

spised of the earth; They who hun - ger and thirst from My hand shall be fed, And their

mourn - ing I'll turn in - to mirth. I will call home the wan - der - ing and

hush their sigh - ing, To My fold they shall come and mourn no more.

Thy Portion.

"Therefore if any man be in Christ, he is a new creature; old things are passed away, behold all things are become new." —2 Cor. v : 17.

Canterbury, N. H.

1. Fel-low trav-'ler, why re-pin-ing? Take with trust thy dai-ly bread. Thou hast
2. Fel-low trav-'ler, no re-pin-ing Shall thy up-ward course de-lay, Thou hast

prayed, the an-swer com-eth: "To the old, the past be dead." Tri-als
Christ to walk be-side thee—Christ, the truth, the life, the way. With thy

search-ing, bat-tles earn-est, Bur-dens heav-y, cross-es sure, Mark the por-tion of the
con-fi-dence un-shak-en, Fill thy heart with courage new; Light, the bur-den God pro-

pil-grim, Till the life in Christ is pure, Till the life in Christ is pure.
vid-eth For the soul with pur-pose true, For the soul with pur-pose true.

The Added Gift.

"For I know that this shall turn to my salvation." — Phil. 1: 19.

Canterbury, N. H.

1. Not e - nough to sing God's praise Un - less my voice may
2. Not e - nough the lambs to feed Un - less my hand may

share, Not e - nough for wis - dom's ways Un - less my feet are there.
move, Not un - less in dai - ly need My heart its love shall prove.

Not e - nough, though all cre - a - tion Bring full sheaves to Zi - on's
Not e - nough, though end - less a - ges Ring the rec - ord of the

store, Not un - less by con - se - cra - tion I am add - ing one gift more.
true, Not un - less on Heav - en's pa - ges Stands my cov - e - nant there - to.

Everlasting Hills.

I will lift up mine eyes unto the hills, from whence cometh my help." — Psa. cxxi: 1.

Canterbury, N. H.

I will lift up mine eyes un - to the hills Whence com - eth my help, whence

com - eth my help. My help com - eth from the Lord, from the Lord of heav'n and earth.

Andante.

He will not suf - fer thy foot to be mov - ed, He that keep - eth thee

will not slum - ber, will not slum - ber. Be - hold He that keep - eth Is - ra - el shall not

tempo.

slum - ber nor sleep, neith - er slum - ber nor sleep. I will lift up mine

whence com - eth

eyes un - to the hills, un - to the hills, the hills, Whence com-eth my help, my

help, whence com - eth my help. My help com - eth from the Lord, from the

Lord of heav'n and earth. He is thy keep - er, He is thy keep - er. The

Lord shall pre - serve thy soul, He shall pre - serve thy go - ing out and thy

com - ing in from this time forth, from this time forth, e - ven for - ev - er more.

74

Sowing.

" Blessed are ye that sow beside all waters."— Isaiah xxxii: 20.

Mt. Lebanon, N. Y.

1. The sun fails not, nor the dews and showers, The sea - sons in their
2. In faith we plant, wait - ing long in prayer, Still trust - ing that the
3. Who toils in love, with an ear - nest heart, His la - bors in the

or - der come and go; So we look in faith to the high - er pow'rs For a
pre-cious seed will live, And bless - ed fruit-age in due time bear. God
Lord are not in vain; The good we here in truth im - part, To the

har-vest from the seed we sow.
sure - ly will the in - crease give. } Let us sow, Let us sow, With a
spir- it will re - turn a - gain.

Let us sow, let us sow,

free and lib-'ral hand; Let us sow, let us sow, O - ver the sea and the land.

Let us sow,

Jerusalem.

"Thou shalt call thy walls Salvation, and thy gates Praise." —Isa. lx : 18.

Canterbury, N. H.

I have build - ed thy tem - ple, I have walled thee a - round, O Je -

ru - sa - lem, With glo - ry and beau - ty I have crowned thee, And I will

pros- per and a - dorn thy Ho - ly Ci - ty, For thou art the Zi - on of God.

Thy gates are praise, thy walls sal - va - tion, Thy streets pure love, and thy

sweet hab - i - ta - tions Are the peace - ful a - bodes of the blest.

Hear My Prayer.

"Evening, and morning, and at noon, will I pray, and he shall hear my voice."— Psa. lv : 17.

Canterbury, N. H.

Hear my prayer, hear my prayer, O Lord, Give ear, give ear to my sup - pli - ca - tion. In Thy faith-ful - ness an - swer me, In Thy faith-ful - ness an - swer me; In the morn - ing will I di - rect my prayer un - to Thee and will look up; for un - to Thee, O Lord, do I lift up my soul. Lead me in Thy right - eous - ness ; make Thy

way straight be-fore me. O - pen Thou my lips to show forth Thy praise.

For Thou de-sir - eth not sac - ri - fice. The sac - ri - fi - ces of God are a

bro - ken spir - it. A bro - ken and con - trite heart, O God, thou wilt not de -

spise. Tru - ly God is good to Is - ra - el. God is good, God is good, is

good to Is - ra - el, e - ven to such as are of a clean heart.

The Christian's Guerdon.

"Surely goodness and mercy shall follow me all the days of my life : and I will dwell in the house of the
Lord forever."— Psa. 23 : 6.

Canterbury, N. H.

1. Thy good-ness hath fol-lowed my life, Thy mer-cies en - com-pass my way ; 'Mid
2. Our God reigns, His law is su-preme, His guid-ance so lov-ing I trace, So

sun-shine, the storm or the strife, God's love ev - er rul - eth the day.
won-drous His power to re - deem, So beau-teous His e - ter - nal grace.

In paths of sweet peace gently led, In ver-dant fields, by liv - ing springs From
My life shall henceforth hon-or Thee, Thy mar-vel - ous con-quests a - dore, With-

God's boun-teous grace rich - ly fed, Tri - umph-ant my soul ev - er sings.
in Thy courts hum - ble and free, I serve Thee, my God, ev - er - more.

The Hymn Eternal.

"Unto thee will I sing, O thou Holy One of Israel."—Psa. lxxi: 22.

Canterbury, N. H.

1. There are notes of joy and beau-ty In my psalm of praise to-
day; There are chords of peace and bless-ing, Sweet-ly blend-ing all the way.
I will add no strain of dis-cord, But at-tune my voice to
prayer, Giv-ing heart and hand in ser-vice, Sing my psalm with trust and care.

2. From my theme of Chris-tian du-ty, Rich in ca-den-ces of
peace, Rise full meas-ures keyed to tri-umph, As the tones of trust in-crease.
Heav'n-ly mel-o-dies I'm sing-ing, U-ni-son with powers on
high, Syl-la-bled the hymn e-ter-nal, In the love that can-not die.

Salvation.

"Fear not: for I am with thee : I will bring thy seed from the east, and gather thee
from the west." — Isa. xliii : 5.

Canterbury, N. H.

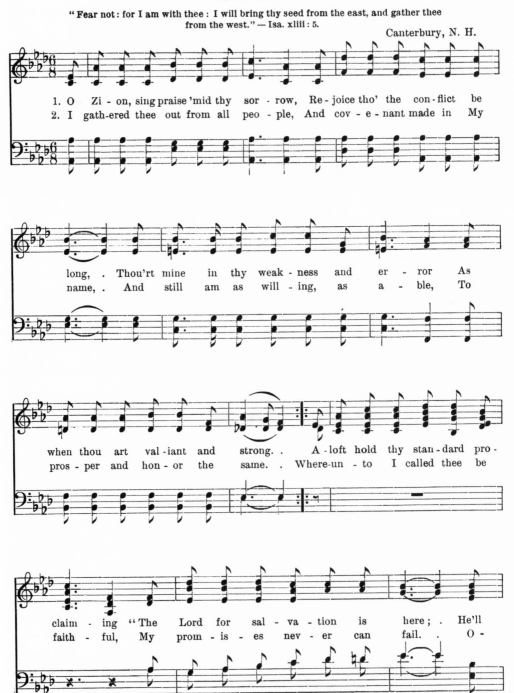

1. O Zi - on, sing praise 'mid thy sor - row, Re - joice tho' the con - flict be
2. I gath-ered thee out from all peo - ple, And cov - e - nant made in My

long, . Thou'rt mine in thy weak - ness and er - ror As
name, . And still am as will - ing, as a - ble, To

when thou art val -iant and strong. . A - loft hold thy stan - dard pro -
pros - per and hon - or the same. . Where-un - to I called thee be

claim - ing "The Lord for sal - va - tion is here ; . He'll
faith - ful, My prom - is - es nev - er can fail. . O -

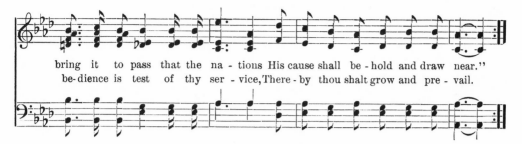

bring it to pass that the na - tions His cause shall be - hold and draw near.''
be - dience is test of thy ser - vice, There - by thou shalt grow and pre - vail.

Landmarks.

"Verily, verily, I say unto you, He that entereth not by the door into the sheepfold, but climbeth up
some other way, the same is a thief and a robber."— St. John x : 1.

Canterbury, N. H.

To the King - dom we're ad - vanc - ing, By the land - marks of our
day; By the low - ly Shep - herd guid - ed, Climb - ing up no oth - er way.
O the rest, the strength of spir - it, Which the flock of Christ en -
joy! Love and peace which they in - her - it Can no stran - ger's voice de - stroy.

Our Passport to Heaven.

"Seek ye first the kingdom of God, and his righteousness."— Matt. vi : 33.

Canterbury, N. H.

1. As we gath-er round the al-tar Ask-ing mer-cy, love and care, As we knock at Heav-en's por-tals, For an-oth-er breathe a prayer, For an-oth-er breathe a prayer. Ask a bless-ing on the shep-herds, Faith-ful guard-ians of the flock; Let our lives be-come es-

2. O re-cord-ing an-gel, lis-ten As thou pass-est in thy flight, Pause and write our names in Heav-en In the ho-ly book of life, In the ho-ly book of life. For by truth and right-eous liv-ing We shall build a man-sion pure. Loy-al ser-vice, free-ly

tab - lished On the true and liv - ing rock, On the true and liv - ing rock.
giv - en, Will our pass - port there in - sure, Will our pass - port there in - sure.

God's Promise.

"According to the word that I covenanted with you when ye came out of Egypt, so my spirit remaineth among you: fear ye not."— Hag. ii: 5.

Canterbury, N. H.

Is - ra - el, thou art not for - sak - en, Where - fore thy peo - ple mourn?

To thy vi - tal in - ter - ests wak - en, To thy song of joy re - turn.

When I brought thee out of E - gypt, All thy sin and grief I knew;

And I prom - ised to sus - tain thee,— More than prom - ised will I do.

Christian Growth.

"Consider the lilies of the field, how they grow."— Matt. vi : 28.

Canterbury, N. H.

1. The vine grow-eth, The stream rolls on its way, 'Tis by
2. Thou seek-est pow-er? Re - pent and sin no more; Growth in

law cre - a - tion mov - eth— Un - chang-ing law that marks God's way.
Chris - tian self - de - ni - al This wise pe - ti - tion will se - cure.

Ear-nest soul, then trust thy prog-ress To the dis - ci - pline of grace, By the
Heav - en hath its seal up - on thee, Light is beam - ing in thy soul; Let this

cross, so close and bind - ing, Comes the strength to run thy race.
truth and peace re - fresh thee, Let this love all fear con - trol.

Bright Vision.

"I press toward the mark for the prize of the high calling of God in Christ Jesus."— Phil. iii: 14.

Canterbury, N. H.

1. There's land be-yond, I see the height, Press on, my soul, nor fear the night, A
2. There's land be-yond, I scale the height That ris - es to my spir - it's sight; In

broad - er truth, a pur - er love Shall guide thee to those realms a - bove.
light and love lose less - er gains To find where Christ in vir - tue reigns.

Tho' oth - er climes at-trac-tions hold, Here's wealth of soul not shrined in gold, Here
A voice from out the "high-er plane," Calls Zi - on to bap-tize a - gain, To

flow'rs di - vine in hal - lowed sod All nur - tured by the hand of God.
live in God in works of truth, In love which o - ver- comes the earth.

Invocation.

"All things, whatsoever ye shall ask in prayer, believing, ye shall receive."— Matt. xxi : 22.

Canterbury, N. H.

1. O list, our Fa - ther, to our prayer, As hum - bly we draw near, We
2. O may Thy ho - ly spir - it rest Up - on this chos - en few ; And

ask Thy strength the feet to guide, Thy love which casts out fear. Take
give us fer - ven - cy of heart, Thy per - fect will to do. We

from us ev - 'ry world - ly strife, And give us sav - ing power To
ask the gift of wis - dom, The pre - cious boon of love, The

cleanse the heart and bring the life To Thee, hence-forth for - ev - er.
chain of spir - it un - ion That links with worlds a - bove.

Heaven's Blessing.

"Prove me now herewith, saith the Lord of hosts, if I will not open the windows of heaven and pour you out a blessing, that there shall not be room enough to receive it."— Mal. iii : 10.

Canterbury, N. H.

I will o-pen the win-dows of heav'n to thee And send forth a bless-ing di-vine, That will clothe thee with wis-dom and crown thee with peace, As mes-sen-gers will-ing of mine. In thy keep-ing are treas-ures of e-ter-nal wealth, Gifts need-ful for thee I pre-pare; Wher-ev-er thy mis-sion doth call thee to serve, My pres-ence shall go with thee there.

My Covenant.

"Arise, shine; for thy light is come."— Isa. lx: 1.

Canterbury, N. H.

A - rise, shine, for thy light is come. A - rise, shine, for thy light, thy light is come, and the glo - ry of the Lord, the glo - ry of the Lord is ris'n . . up - on thee. I, the Lord have call - ed thee, have call - ed thee in right - eous-ness and will keep thee, and will keep . . thee and give thee for a cov - e - nant, a cov - e - nant of the peo - ple.

Thou shalt be call - ed by a new name, Thou shalt be call - ed

by a new name, by a new name which the mouth of the Lord shall name.

O come ye, O come . . ye, O come let us walk in the

light,

light of the Lord, In the light of the Lord, let us walk in the light, in the

light . . of the Lord. I will men - tion the prais - es of the

My Covenant.

Lord,   the prais - es, the prais - es   of the Lord, the Lord. My soul shall be

of the Lord,

joy - ful, my soul shall be joy - ful,   be joy - ful   in   my God.

Passport.

"Let the heart of them rejoice that seek the Lord." — 1 Chron. xvi : 10.

Canterbury, N. H.

I am sure of my pass - port, Al - read - y I see The land of bright

prom - ise Is   o - pen to me.   Re - joice and sing prais - es   In

work well be - gun, For rich the pos - ses - sion When full vic - t'ry's won.

Consecration.

"Now ye have consecrated yourselves unto the Lord." — 2 Chron. xxix : 31.

Harvard, Mass. Canterbury, N. H.

1. Here's my heart, to God I give it, Voice and tongue to praise His name;
2. I've a con-science thus pro-tect-ed, Worth a throne and di-a-dem;
3. I have feet, with God they're walk-ing, For with gos-pel peace they're shod;
4. I have ears to hear the sto-ry Men and an-gels love to tell;

I have life, to Him I live it,—Hands, to Him de-vote the same.
I've a man-sion well se-lect-ed In the New Je-ru-sa-lem.
Most fa-mil-iar-ly I'm talk-ing As I take my walk with God.
Eyes, to see the ris-ing glo-ry Which shall Zi-on's tri-umph swell.

I've a field, to sow and reap it, And must reap what-e'er it grows;
Hence, I have in this con-nec-tion Thus pre-pared, a hap-py home;
I have thought, the great-est treas-ure That the u-ni-verse can sing;
I have pray'r, to God I make it, While mine eye His throne sur-veys;

I've a par-a-dise, I'll keep it, For it blos-soms as the rose.
Such a home, that my af-fec-tion Does not, will not, can-not roam.
There is no ma-te-rial treas-ure Which can such pos-ses-sions bring.
I've a gold-en harp, I'll wake it, To a song of end-less praise.

Voice of Song.

"I will sing unto the Lord because he hath dealt bountifully with me." — Psa. xiii : 6.

Canterbury, N. H.

1. O sing with joy, and let thy song Of grat - i - tude and prayer As -
2. For bless - ings o'er thy path - way strewn, Rich mer - cies man - i - fold, Give
3. O sing of ho - ly friendships blest, God's good - ness free - ly given, Of

cend in glad - ness from thy soul, For God's great love and care.
thanks, my soul, in hum - ble praise, God's gifts in hon - or hold.
love, of home, true hap - pi - ness, A - bid - ing peace, and heav'n.

O sing, and let the voice of song Rise high o'er crest - ed

wave, For Christ the Lord has come to reign, With pow'r divine to save.

high o'er crested wave, For

Blessed be the Lord.

"The Lord is my strength: He is the saving strength of his anointed." — Psa. xxviii: 8.

Canterbury, N. H.

Un-to Thee, O Lord, do I lift up my soul, Un-to Thee, O Lord, do I

lift up my soul; O God, I trust, I trust in Thee, O God, I trust, I

Show me Thy ways, O Lord,

trust in Thee. Show me Thy ways, O Lord, Show me Thy

Show me Thy ways, O Lord,

ways, O Lord, Teach me, teach me, teach me Thy paths, Show me Thy

ways, O Lord, show me Thy ways, O Lord, and teach me Thy paths.

Lead me in Thy truth and teach . . me, Lead me in Thy truth and

teach . me . . for Thou art the God of my sal - va - - tion,

Thou art the God of my sal - va - - tion, on Thee do I wait, I

wait all the day. Re - mem - ber, O Lord, Thy ten - der mer-cies and Thy

lov - ing kind-ness, Thy ten - der mer - cies and Thy lov - ing kind - ness, for

they have been ev - er of old. They have been ev - er, been ev - er of old.

Bless - ed be the Lord, Bless - ed be the Lord, . . The

Lord is my strength; He is the sav - ing strength of His a - noint - ed.

Save Thy peo - ple, save Thy peo - ple and bless Thine in - her - i - tance;

feed and lift them up, feed . . them and lift them up for - ev - er.

The Promised Comforter.

"He shall give you another Comforter, that he may abide with you forever." — John xiv : 16.

Canterbury, N. H.

If ye love Me, keep My commandments, keep My com-mand-ments, And I will
pray the Fa-ther and He shall give you a Com-fort-er, that He may a-

The Spir-it of Truth, ... of
bide with you for-ev - er. The Spir-it of Truth, the
The Spir-it of
the

Truth, ...
Spir-it of Truth, that He may a-bide with you for-ev-er.
Truth, of Truth,
Spir-it of Truth,

If ye love Me, keep My com-mand-ments, If ye love Me,

keep My com-mand-ments; And I will pray the Fa - ther and He shall give you a

Com-fort - er, E - ven the Spir - it of Truth, that He may a - bide with

you for - ev - er. I will not leave you com - fort - less, I will not

leave you com - fort - less; He shall give you, shall give you an - oth - er

Com-fort-er, that He may a - bide with you, a - bide for - ev - er.

My Saviour.

"For he taught as one having authority, and not as the scribes."—Matt. vii: 29.

Canterbury, N. H.

1. How ex-alt-ed and how beau-ti-ful, the say-ings of our
2. Though ut-tered a-ges long a-go, they still re-tain the
3. My .. Sav-iour, O, I love Thy life, so free from guile and

Lord! How clothed in grace and dig-ni-ty, is each in-spir-ed
power To cheer the wea-ry soul, and throw light o'er each ad-verse
stain; Thy in-no-cence and pu-ri-ty my ad-o-ra-tion

word! They are to me as gold-en fruit, in sil-ver pict-ures
hour; And count-less mil-lions, a-ges hence, shall sing and speak the
claim. It serves to el-e-vate my mind to count Thy vir-tues

set, Like mu-sic which the fi-nite voice can nev-er coun-ter-feit.
praise, Which fills the heart and moves the lips of saints in lat-ter days.
o'er, And prompts the strife to pat-tern Thee,—to "go and sin no more."

Humble Petition.

"He is our God ; and we are the people of his pasture and the sheep of his hand." — Psa. xcv: 7.

Canterbury, N. H.

1. Breathe on our souls, O Lord, we pray The strength'ning power of faith; Ar-
2. As we in-voke Thy fa - vor, Lord, O may we live to Thee; And

rest our foot-steps in the way That lead-eth down to death. For
while we trust Thy way and word, More con-se-crat-ed be! We

what is life with-out Thy grace To mould each liv-ing act? And
would be will-ing in-stru-ments, De-pen-dent on Thy will. We

what is joy with-out the smile Of God to ap-pro-bate?
would re-flect Thy pow'r, Thy love, And thus our call ful-fill.

Voice of Supplication.

"Give ear, O Lord, unto my prayer, and attend to the voice of my supplication." — Psa. lxxxvi: 6.

Canterbury, N. H.

There is a treas - ure, There is a treas - ure, a treas - ure to be de -

There is a treas - ure to be de - sired,

sired, the sa - cred gift of God, the peace of right-eous-ness, the

Light of Life, the glo - ry of our God, the glo - ry of our God.

Seek by prayer, by prayer and sup-pli-ca - tion the best gifts, and God shall hear thy pray'r.

Give ear, O Shep-herd of Is - ra - el, turn to us a - gain and cause Thy

face to shine up-on us and we shall be sav-ed. Give ear, O Lord, un-to my

prayer, and at-tend to the voice of my sup-pli-ca-tion. One

thing have I de-sir-ed of the Lord, that will I seek. That I may

dwell in the house of the Lord all the days . of my life to be-

days, all the days of my life.

hold the beau-ty of the Lord, and to en-quire in His tem-ple. For in

time of trou - ble He shall hide me, He shall hide me in His pa -

vil - ion, in the se - cret of His tab - er - na - cle shall He hide me.

Forgiveness.

"If ye forgive not men their trespasses, neither will your Father forgive your trespasses." — Matt. vi : 15.

Canterbury, N. H.

O shall I for - give? "For - give and be for - giv - en; Where

love does not tar - ry Our God can - not reign. His arm is sal - va - tion, His

love is a ref - uge, — A ref - uge, for the err - ing And a rest for the strong."

Daily Blessings.

"His compassions fail not. They are new every morning."— Lam. iii : 22, 23.

Canterbury, N. H.

As new ev - 'ry morn-ing Thy mer - cies de - scend, And bless-ings so

rich crown each day, Free, free from the fount of Thy good-ness I drink,— Thy

truth is my shield and my stay. My life ev - er guid - ed by

coun - sel di - vine, While strength for each du - ty is giv'n, In glad-ness of

heart my thanksgiv - ing as - cends,— A sac - ri - fice new un - to heav'n.

Freedom.

"Is not this that I have chosen? to undo the heavy burdens, and to let the oppressed go free?"—
Isaiah lviii: 6.

Canterbury, N. H.

1. Is there a faint heart that hun - gers, An eye that would more clear-ly see?
2. Lon - ger thine heart shall not hun - ger, Thine eye shall be sin - gle and true.

Is there a foot - fall that lin - gers, Un - cer - tain the mis - sion to be?
For - ward thy foot - steps shall has - ten, With ho - li - er pros-pects in view.

Is there a bur - den op - pres - sive The toil - er would glad - ly lay down? O
Ac - cents of sa - cred con - vic - tion Im-press thee as mes-sage di - vine; The

bey the still voice of the Spir - it And free-dom thine ef - forts shall crown.
Spir - it hath sealed thee for du - ty, Thy life to its coun-sel re - sign.

My Passport.

"Your life is hid with Christ in God."—Col. iii: 3.

Canterbury, N. H.

1. I seek a heav'n-ly treas-ure, A her-i-tage se-cure, A life by sin un-tar-nished, The pass-port of the pure. I seek the hal-lowed mis-sion To scat-ter truth a-broad, Would know full con-se-cra-tion, Un-bro-ken vows to God.

2. Wilt thou with-in the shad-ow Of Christ the Rock be hid? Be lost to self-ish in-t'rests, Serve as our Sav-iour did? Go work a-mong my need-y, Give to the least of mine. In hum-ble min-is-tra-tion Re-demp-tion shall be thine.

Sing unto God.

"All the earth shall worship thee, and shall sing to thy name." — Psa. lxvi: 4.

Canterbury, N. H.

Sing un-to God, O ye kingdoms of the earth; O sing prais-es un-

to the Lord. Sing forth the hon-ors of His name, make His praise glo-ri-ous.

En-ter in-to His gates with thanksgiv-ing and in-to His courts with praise, Be

thank-ful un-to Him and bless His name, Be thank-ful un-to

Him and bless .. His name, and bless His name.

He is our God, of whom com-eth sal - va - tion; For Thou, Lord, art good and

gra - cious, and of great mer - cy, of great . . mer-cy un - to all, to

all that call up -on Thee, For Thou, Lord, art good and
That call on Thee,

gra - cious and of great mer - cy un - to all, to all them that

call, ... that call up - on . . Thee. I will praise the Lord, I will

Sing unto God.

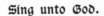

praise the Lord and will sing . . praise to the name of the Lord, Most High.

My Choice.

"Ye seek me, not because ye saw the miracles, but because ye did eat of the loaves, and were filled." —
St. John vi: 26.

Canterbury, N. H.

For more than loaves as gifts I serve, Thy work, Thy life, Thy

cross I love ; Of choice I fol - low in Thy way, For Thou art my sal - va - tion. Thou

art my guide, my po - lar star, Thy mer - cies bless and shine a - far, In -

vit - ing age and call - ing youth To share the blest re - la - tion

Call of the Spirit.

"Come unto me all ye that labor and are heavy laden, and I will give you rest."—Matt. xi: 28.

Canterbury, N. H.

1. My soul hears the ech - o of the Spir - it that calls,
2. Ah, I will not lin - ger my Sav - iour to heed But

"Come un - to Me and find rest, My yoke is easy, and my bur - den is light," And
trust - ing - ly fol - low each day, Wher-e'er He leads me, what-ev - er approves, His

those who ac - cept will be blest. O seek then the gifts that the
lov - ing com - mands I'll o - bey. True joy greets the soul in the

Spir - it doth hold, True love, joy, the soul's deep - est peace, Give,
strait, nar - row way, E - ter - nal em - ploy - ment and rest, I

Call of the Spirit.

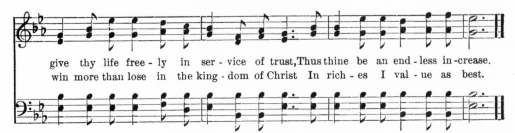

give thy life free - ly in ser - vice of trust, Thus thine be an end - less in - crease.
win more than lose in the king - dom of Christ In rich - es I val - ue as best.

Sun of Righteousness.

"The Lord shall be unto thee an everlasting light, and thy God thy glory."—Isa. lx : 19.

Canterbury, N. H.

In the spir - it - ual sky there is beam - ing A sun that will nev - er go

down; O'er the hill-tops its light is stream - ing, Re - veal - ing the e - ter - nal morn.

E'en the arch - es of heav - en are shin - ing, And the path of the pil - grim is

bright; All dark clouds have a sil - ver lin - ing From the orb - it of truth and right.

My Psalm.

"Do not cease to pray and to desire that ye might be filled with the knowledge of his will, in all wisdom and spiritual understanding."— Col. i: 9.

Canterbury, N. H.

Pa - tient and faith -ful, yet joy -ful my soul, Ask - ing in all things that

wis-dom con -trol; Guard-ed art thou by an Arm safe and strong, Truth as thy

ref - uge, and faith thy "New Song." Hal-lowed thy trust,—let its wings bear thee

on To heights grand-ly ris -ing as vic - t'ries are won Op-'ning new pa - ges of

life, joy and peace, A heav - en-crowned home tho' its meas-ures in - crease.

Protection.

"Ye are of more value than many sparrows."— Matt. **x** : 31.

Canterbury, N. H.

Our God who marks the spar-row's fall, Will hear my earn-est pray'r, And bless with strength to heed the call The Sav-iour's cross, the Sav-iour's cross to bear. Tho' on-ly one a-mong the least, I know the Shep-herd's voice, And where He leads in paths of peace, I'll fol-low, I'll fol-low free of choice.

Life's Meaning.

"So teach us to number our days, that we may apply our hearts unto wisdom."— Psa. xc: 12.

Canterbury, N. H.

1. What is life and what its mean - ing? Oft the sol - emn tho't ap -
2. Blessed with strength and zeal for ac - tion, Christ or mam - mon we must

pears; We have hearts and souls for heav - eu, Hands that wea - ry with the
choose; For the glo - ry of our Mak - er, May we all our tal - ents

years. A - gen - cy so free and ac - tive—Shall we choose, re - fuse the true? God's rich
use. Life's brief page is heaven's ser - mon, Let us read its lines with care, Trace earth's

gift this life is pass - ing; Ours to claim with rev - 'rence due.
plan in lov - ing ser - vice, Thus the heaven - ly pros-pects share.

Sowing to the Spirit.

"The wilderness and the solitary place shall be glad for them." — Isa. xxxv: 1.

Canterbury, N. H.

1. While sow-ing by the way - side Or oft in gar - dens fair, O scat- ter thoughts of
2. The lan-guage of the ho - ly Ex-pressed in guile-less speech, A lan-guage chaste and

glad - ness And bless-ing ev - 'ry - where, In words of peace and prof - it, In
come - ly, May we em-brace and teach. For more than treas-ures earth - ly Our

deeds of love and care, That wil -der-ness and des - ert May bloom with har - vest
souls as - pire to gain, That ex-ceed-ing weight of glo - ry In the bliss- ful words: "Well

rare, That wil - der - ness and des - ert May bloom with har - vest rare.
done," That ex - ceed - ing weight of glo - ry In the bliss - ful words:" Well done."

Spirit World.

"Behold, the kingdom of God is within you."— Luke xvii: 21.

Canterbury, N. H.

1. Bright Spir - it World, bright land of souls, Art thou a - bove the
2. O pil - grim, list, look not a - far,— Be - low nor yet a -

stars? Hast thou for me im- mor- tal bliss, No grief nor sigh that mars? And will the
bove; The spir - it world is Truth and Light, Is Mer - cy, Peace and Love. And as these

friends who loved me here Still know me as I pass? And shall I
gifts thy life con - trol Thou hast "thy king-dom come," E - ter - nal

hear the wel-come song Ring o'er the "Sea of Glass," Ring o'er the "Sea of Glass?"
life, en - dur - ing bliss, With kin-dred souls a home, With kin-dred souls a home.

Rejoice.

"All nations whom thou hast made shall come and worship before thee, and shall glorify thy name." — Psalm lxxxvi: 9.

Canterbury, N. H.

O sing to the Lord, all ye lands, Sing! Re-joice in the good-ness of God. Re-

Sing . . . . . to God;

joice, all ye na - tions, and sing and be glad, sing and be glad; Re-

Sing . . . . . to God, and glo - ri - fy His name

joice in the goodness of God. Glo-ri - fy His name for - ev - er more.

For great is the Lord, and of great pow'r; His un-derstand-ing is in - fi - nite;

Right - eous and upright are His judg-ments; His word is ver - y pure, There-fore His

ser-vant lov - eth it. His right-eous - ness is an ev - er - last-ing righteousness,

and His law is the truth. Save us, O Lord our God, And gather us to give

thanks to Thy ho - ly name and to tri - umph in Thy praise.

Alfred, Me.

Let Zi - on move as the heart of one, Her light shine forth as the

ris - ing sun, And let her peo - ple all become Bap-tized with fire from heav - en.

Send ho - ly in - spi - ra - tion down; Heav'nly Fa - ther, from Thy throne,

Leave, O . . leave us not a - lone, An - gel guides di - rect us.

Unto Me.

"Inasmuch as ye have done it unto one of the least of these, ye have done it unto me."— Matt. xxv : 40.

Canterbury, N. H.

1. Has the cup of cold wa - ter been giv - en to - day? Have the need - y been
2. Has the wan- d'rer been sought and for - giv - en to - day? With those who would

fed? Were the lame turned a - way? The Sav -iour now stands in our midst!
harm did'st thou ear - nest - ly pray? The Sav - iour has trav - ersed the way.

His mer - ci - ful teach - ing is search - ing the ways Of
His ho - ly com - pas - sion has light - ed the dark - ness, And

those who to Him would bring hon- or and praise, Say-ing "Give to the least and ye
down thro' the a - ges He call - eth to thee, Say-ing "Give to the least and ye

give un - to Me, Give, give   to   the   least and ye give un - to Me."

After the Storm.

"And the work of righteousness shall be peace; and the effect of righteousness quietness and assurance
for ever."— Isa. xxxii: 17.

Canterbury, N. H.

When storms have passed, with for - ces spent, And yet   I   firm - ly stand, Deep

rest a - bid - ing in   the   soul, Comes   by   the scourg - ing   hand.

Still wise and hum - ble, O   my soul, No day   can be too long   To

fill with deeds of   love and truth, In prayer, in   praise or   song.

Intercession.

"Pray ye therefore the Lord of the harvest that he will send forth laborers into his harvest." — Matt. ix: 38.

Canterbury, N. H.

1. Bap - tize with the pow'r of the world to come, Fill us with Thy light di -
2. En - light - en the ma - ny who're wait-ing to see Whith-er doth Thy spir - it

vine; O - pen the foun-tains of truth for we thirst, Make us dis - ci - ples of Thine.
draw; O - pen their hearts to a knowledge of Thee, With pow'r to o - bey Thy law.

Has - ten the time when the la - bor - ers shall be Ma - ny in Thy vine-yard,
Broad is the field and the gold - en har - vest waits, Need - y is Thy vine-yard,

Lord, Sow -ing and reap-ing the har-vest for Thee, Filled with the love of Thy word.
Lord, Send to our aid ac - tive workers for Thee, Filled with the pow'r of Thy word.

Assurance.

"He commandeth even the winds and water, and they obey him." — Luke viii : 25.

Canterbury, N. H.

1. I have launched up - on life's o - cean, In God's love and mer - cy
2. I can sing up - on life's o - cean Christ, my Pi - lot, ev - er

sure, To the res - ur - rec - tion heav - ens, I am sail - ing with the pure.
near. As I trust His wise di - rec - tion, Earth - ly dan - gers dis - ap - pear.

Do not talk to me of ship-wreck; With the Lord I shall pre -
Prayer is proof a - gainst dis - as - ter, As I stem the might - y

vail, Pass in safe - ty trou-bled wa - ters, Har - bor in Re - demption's Vale.
wave; Storm and cloud but prove my cour - age, Is - rael's God is strong to save.

The Lord is Gracious.

"Gracious is the Lord, and righteous ; yea, our God is merciful."—Psa. cxvi : 5.

Canterbury, N. H.

The Lord is gra - cious and right - eous, yea, our God is mer - ci - ful.

Gra - cious is the Lord, Gra - cious is the Lord, Gra - cious is the Lord, and

Our God

right-eous ; The Lord our God is mer - ci - ful, our God is mer - ci - ful.

Be strong, and let your heart take cour-age, all ye that hope, that hope in the Lord,

Wor- ship the Lord in the beau - ty of ho - li - ness, Wor- ship the Lord in the

beau - ty of ho - li - ness, The beau - ty of ho - li - ness, of ho - li - ness. The

Lord will give strength un - to His peo - ple, The Lord will give strength un -

to His peo - ple. The Lord will bless, will bless His peo - ple with

peace, with peace, will bless with peace. Give un - to the Lord the
the Lord

glo - ry due un - to His name. Give, give un - to the Lord glo - ry and strength.

The Lord is Gracious.

Un - to the Lord, un - to the Lord give glo - ry and strength.

Compassion.

"I came not to call the righteous but sinners to repentance."— Luke v : 32.

Canterbury, N. H.

Call the need - y chil - dren home, make a feast that they may share;

Not the world - ly wise and whole need the Good Phy - si - cian's care.

'Tis the mis - sion of God's love to re - claim, re - store, re - deem,

Give full in - terest, joy and love, life and la - bor to this theme.

The Life=Boat.

"If God be for us, who can be against us?" — Rom. viii: 31.

Canterbury, N. H.

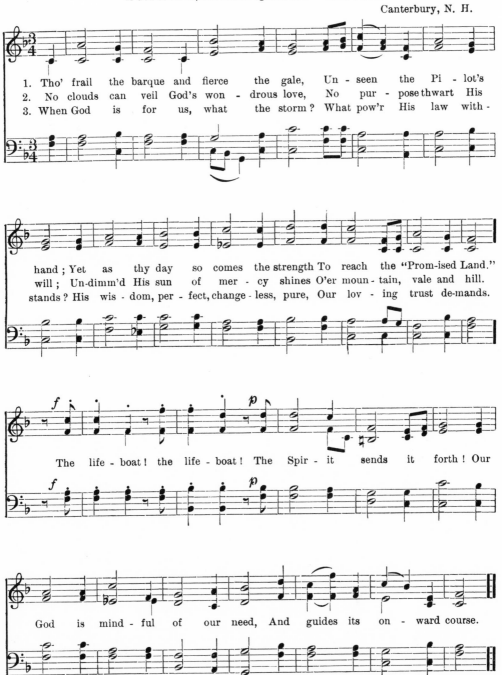

1. Tho' frail the barque and fierce the gale, Un - seen the Pi - lot's
2. No clouds can veil God's won - drous love, No pur - pose thwart His
3. When God is for us, what the storm? What pow'r His law with -

hand; Yet as thy day so comes the strength To reach the "Prom-ised Land."
will; Un-dimm'd His sun of mer - cy shines O'er moun - tain, vale and hill.
stands? His wis - dom, per - fect, change - less, pure, Our lov - ing trust de-mands.

The life - boat! the life - boat! The Spir - it sends it forth! Our

God is mind - ful of our need, And guides its on - ward course.

The Lord Reigneth.

"Sing, O heavens; and be joyful, O earth; for the Lord hath comforted his people." — Isaiah xlix : 13.

Canterbury, N. H.

The Lord reign-eth! Let the heav'ns re - joice, let the earth be glad, and let all that is there - in bless His ho - ly name. All na - tions shall come and wor-ship be - fore Thee, O Lord, our God, and shall glo - ri - fy Thy name.

For Thou art plen-teous in mer - cy un - to all them that call up - on Thee. Thou hast been a strength to the poor and need - y, a ref - uge, a

ref - uge from the storm. We have wait - ed for Thee, we have wait - ed for

Thee, Thou wilt save us, wilt save us, wilt save us with Thy

glo - ri - ous sal - va - tion. O Lord, in Thee do I put my trust, I will

pay Thee my vows. I will of - fer un - to Thee the sac - ri -

fi - ces of thanksgiv - ing, and I will de - clare what Thou hast done for my

soul, for my soul. Hear my pray'r, O God, hear my pray'r, turn Thou

un - to me ac - cord-ing to the mul - ti - tude of Thy ten - der mer - cies.

All Thy works shall praise Thee and Thy saints shall bless Thee ; Thy

pow'r and great goodness shall they make known and shall sing of Thy right-eous-ness, for

Thou art our God, Thou art from ev - er - last - ing to ev - er - last - ing.

The Christ Work.

"For the Son of man is come to seek and to save that which was lost." — Luke xix : 10.

Canterbury, N. H.

1. I will lead you, I will feed you, I will help you a-
2. I will hear you, I will cheer you, As a Com-fort-er

long; Let no tem-pest give you bur-den, Shade or sad-den your song;
nigh; Fal-ter nev-er, trust-ing ev-er, Strength is yours from on high;

For my mis-sion, sa-cred mis-sion, Is to gath-er the
For I give un-to the an-gels Charge con-cern-ing the

lost — Call-ing sin-ners to re-pent-ance, Nev-er count-ing the cost.
true; Ev-'ry foot-fall shall be cour-age, All the way to pur-sue.

Daily Praise.

"Every day will I bless thee ; and I will praise thy name for ever and ever."— Psa. cxlv : 2.

Canterbury, N. H.

1. O sing in the morning the bless- ing of peace, O sing ye at noon-day when
2. O sing 'mid the shad-ows, tho' of - ten they stray ; O sing in the sun-shine that

tri - als in - crease ; Sing, sing as time pass - es, the cross yields a song, The
bright -ens our way. Sing, sing and the an - gels of God ev - er nigh Shall

bur-den ye bear brings re-ward rich and strong. All sing - ing, no mourn-ing, the
bear the re-frain to our Fa - ther on high. All praise, all thanks-giv -ing, all

hours of our God As riv - ers are full, there blos-soms the rod. No sor-row can
joy shall as -cend, For mer-cies so great, for life with-out end, For hon - or, for

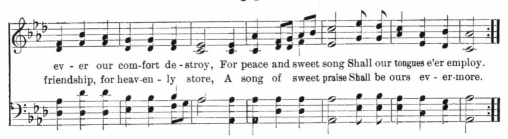

ev - er our com-fort de - stroy, For peace and sweet song Shall our tongues e'er employ.

friendship, for heav-en - ly store, A song of sweet praise Shall be ours ev - er-more.

Loyalty.

"O the depth of the riches both of the wisdom and knowledge of God."— Rom. xi: 33.

Canterbury, N. H.

O Zi - on, thy growth is my care, Oth - er in- t'rests I free - ly re -

sign, Most hum-bly thy bur - den to bear And con-se-crate all at thy shrine.

The rich- ness of bless- ing I know In treas- ures that fade not a -

way, Sur-pass all that earth can be - stow, The her-ald of e - ter-nal day.

Petition.

"Before they call, I will answer; and while they are yet speaking, I will hear."— Isa. lxv: 24.

Canterbury, N. H.

O Source of light, of truth, and love, We come to Thee this hour, To
ask a-gain for love and strength, Thine all - sus - tain - ing power.

O'er ev - 'ry self - ish el - e - ment We seek di - vine con -
trol; O may Thy in - spi - ra - tion pure Fill ev - 'ry need - y soul.

Prayer for the Nations.

"The earth shall be filled with the knowledge of the glory of the Lord, as the waters cover the sea."—
Habak. ii: 14.

Canterbury, N. H.

1. O God of mer - cy, truth and love, We hum - bly ask of
2. For the heal - ing of the na - tions Most fer - vent - ly we

Thee, To turn each heart from sin and strife, To set the na - tions
pray That peace on earth, good - will to men O'er all the earth bear

free. Cause peace to rule and wars to cease, Which do so sore op -
sway. In - spire each heart with liv - ing faith, Thy pre - cepts to o -

press, For the heal - ing of the na - tions, O God, draw nigh to bless.
bey, For the heal - ing of the na - tions, Lord, has - ten Thou the day.

Eternal Goodness.

"The earth is full of the goodness of the Lord."— Psa. xxxiii : 5.

Canterbury, N. H.

The earth is the Lord's and the ful - ness there-of, The earth is the Lord's and the

The world . . . . . .

ful - ness there - of, The world and they that dwell there-in, The

world and they that dwell there - in. Of old hast Thou laid the foun -

da - tion of the earth and the heav - ens, the heav - ens are the

work of Thy hands. They shall per - ish but Thou shalt en - dure; all of

them shall wax old like a gar- ment. As a ves - ture shalt Thou change them and

they shall be changed. But Thou art the same, Thy years have no end,

Thou art the same, Thy years have no end. How man - i -fold are Thy works,

O Lord! In Thy wis - dom hast Thou made them all ; The earth is

full of Thy rich - es, Thou send - est forth Thy spir - it, Thou re -

Eternal Goodness.

new - est the face of the earth; Ev - en from ev - er - last - ing to

ev - er - last - ing Thou art God, our Shield, our Ref-uge, our Strength, our High Tow'r.

My Kingdom.

"And the smoke of the incense, which came with the prayers of the saints, ascended up before God." — Rev. viii : 4.

Canterbury, N. H.

My kingdom's not di - vid - ed Nor will my peo - ple stray, In Me have they con-

fid - ed And made My law their stay. Their sac - ri - fi - ces ho - ly As

incense sweet a - rise. Oh, I will bless them tru - ly, They shall not miss the prize.

Holy Spirit.

"Wash me, and I shall be whiter than snow."— Psa. li: 7.

Canterbury, N. H.

I would rath-er win a pure white spir - it, Fit tem-ple for the Ho - ly

Ghost to dwell, . . Than gar-ner earth-ly stores with-out lim - it, The.

rich - es of which vain man can tell. I would give these gifts due con - sid - er -

a - tion, But be-ware lest they gain the con-trol; . . For, when

weighed a-gainst my soul's sal - va - tion, They per-ish as an un-mean-ing scroll.

Psalm of Joy.

"Let them that love thy name be joyful in thee."—Psa. v: 11.

Canterbury, N. H.

Let all those that put their trust in Thee re - joice, Let all those that put their

trust in Thee re - joice, Let them ev - er shout for joy. Let all those that put their

trust in Thee re-joice, Let them that love Thy name be joy - ful in Thee, O

Lord, our Lord. How ex - cel-lent is Thy name in all the earth, in all the earth !

Let all those that seek Thee re - joice and be glad in Thee, Let

Let all those that seek Thee rejoice, rejoice and be glad in Thee,

all those

Let those that seek Thee re-joice,   Let those that love Thy name be glad,   Let

Let all those

all   those that seek Thee re-joice, Let all   those that love Thy name be   glad ;   For Thy

mer - cy   is great un-to the   heavens   and Thy   truth un-to   the   clouds.

We will sing   and   praise Thy pow'r,   we will sing and praise Thy pow'r for-

ev - er   and for-ev - er, for-ev - er   and   for - ev - er,   for-

Psalm of Joy.

ev - er and for - ev - er,   for - ev - er and for - ev - er   more.

Steadfast.

"For where your treasure is, there will your heart be also."—Matt. vi: 21.

Canterbury, N. H.

All else will fail, seek heav'n's fair land, Its beau - ties can - not die; Se -

cure - ly build with heart and hand And sin - gle keep thine eye.

Stead - fast thy gaze on the glo - rious height, Near - er ap - proach each

day; The ris - en sun which hath no night Will bear all mists a - way.

Let Me Be There.

"These are they which came out of great tribulation, and have washed their robes, and made them white in the blood of the Lamb."— Rev. vii: 14.

Canterbury, N. H.

Let me be there with the ho - ly in heart, With the loy - al on Mount Zi - on stand; Let me be one where the just have a part In the beau - ti - ful wise vir - gin band. Though my whole life it may cost me to gain The height where my soul fain would dwell; Yet if no - bly true to the vows I pro -claim, I'm cer- tain my joy will be full.

Incense.

" If ye then be risen with Christ, seek those things which are above."—Col. iii : 1.

Canterbury, N. H.

1. Leave a-while the things that per-ish, Let the mind and soul o-
2. Ho-ly themes of truth at-tract us, Leave we glad-ly things of

bey; Come en-joy the gifts that nour-ish Nor with us-ing pass a-
time, These an-noy but test the spir-it —Step-ping-stones to heights di-

way, Nor with us-ing pass a-way. Sa-cred prayer as in-cense
vine, Step-ping-stones to heights di-vine. Prayer is sol-ace; waves of

ho-ly Ris-ing, cir-cling in-to light, Now re-turn-ing, rich with
bless-ing Swell in an-swer full and high; Here we trust, though cour-age

prom - ise, Granting fruits which nev - er blight, Grant-ing fruits which nev - er blight.
fal - ter, Here is heard the spar-row's cry, Here is heard the spar - row's cry.

Prayer.

" All things, whatsoever ye shall ask in prayer, believing, ye shall receive." — Matt. xxi: 22.

Canterbury, N. H.

Fa - ther, list; our souls are plead -ing That Thy strength be ev - er nigh;

Meet our ear - nest in - ter - ced - ing, With Thy spir - it from on high.

Of all bless - ings, grant the power Thy all - right - eous way to teach,

And with mer - cy guide the mes - sage That the souls of men will reach.

Light.

West Gloucester, Me.

"Thou shalt guide me with thy counsel."— Psa. lxxiii: 24.

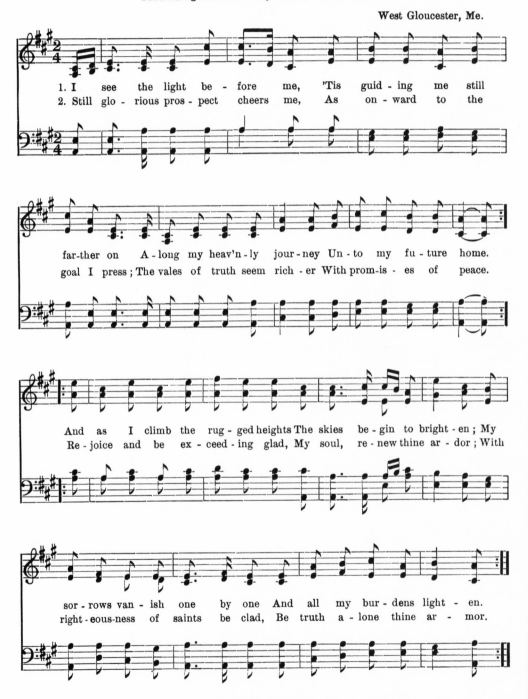

1. I see the light be - fore me, 'Tis guid - ing me still far-ther on A - long my heav'n - ly jour-ney Un - to my fu - ture home.

2. Still glo - rious pros - pect cheers me, As on - ward to the goal I press; The vales of truth seem rich - er With prom-is - es of peace.

And as I climb the rug - ged heights The skies be - gin to bright - en; My sor - rows van - ish one by one And all my bur - dens light - en.

Re - joice and be ex - ceed - ing glad, My soul, re - new thine ar - dor; With right - eous-ness of saints be clad, Be truth a - lone thine ar - mor.

Stewardship.

"Give an account of thy stewardship." — Luke xvi: 2.

Canterbury, N. H.

1. Be lift - ed up, my soul, Till the heav - ens shine up - on thee, And
2. Be lift - ed up, my soul, Catch the glo - ry all a - bove thee, Thy

in the maj - es - ty of truth and love, Thou art a - ble to walk.
ref - uge in ad - ver - si - ty and loss, Is thy Sav - iour, thy God.

Thou shalt set no bounds for la - bor, But as a stew - ard
Let no pow'r of earth en - fee - ble Thy ev - er - last - ing

faith - ful, In God's ser - vice shall thy life In un - ceas - ing meas - ure flow.
pur - pose; In the mem - o - ries of heav'n Be thy stew - ard - ship en - rolled.

Shield.

"Neither is he that planteth anything, neither is he that watereth; but God that giveth the increase."—
1 Cor. iii : 7.

Canterbury, N. H.

1. Live, my soul, as peace shall fol - low And thine ev - 'ry walk con - trol, Here-in
2. In the quest of life e - ter - nal, Leav-ing grief and sin be - hind, God is

lies thy shield from sor - row, Here thy strength for growth of soul, Here thy
cour - age, love and mer - cy, Here thy heart's af - fec - tions bind, Here thy

strength for growth of soul. When thou go - est to the bat - tle, Gos - pel
heart's af - fec - tions bind. Trust His guid - ance all the jour - ney, What-so -

truth shall mark thy way, God may chas - ten, God may chas - ten; Let thy
e'er thy needs af - ford, Know the in - crease of the spir - it As ye

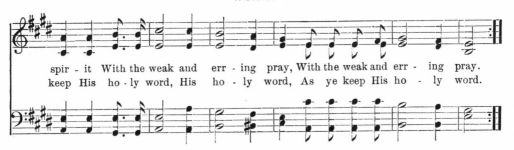

spir - it With the weak and err - ing pray, With the weak and err - ing pray.
keep His ho - ly word, His ho - ly word, As ye keep His ho - ly word.

Guidance.

"No flesh shall glory in his presence."—1 Cor. i: 29.

Canterbury, N. H.

I have led you, my be - lov - ed, To the know-ledge of my

way, Strait as strait-ness, pure as heav - en, To the dawn of end - less day.

In this light no flesh shall glo - ry: Thro all hours of Chris - tian

test, Truth un - fail - ing, just and ho - ly, Is thy stong-hold, joy and rest.

Virgin Church.

"A glorious church, not having spot, or wrinkle, or any such thing." — Eph. v: 27.

Canterbury, N. H.

1. O Vir - gin Church, how great thy light, What cloud can dim thy
2. Not by the creeds or laws of man Hast thou been blest to
can
been

way ! Thou hast the ev - er - last - ing truth That saves all who o - bey.
stand ; God bro't thee forth by Spir - it pow'r And stays thee with His hand.

dim thy way !
blest to stand ;

The Christ is thy e - ter - nal law, A sure and safe re - pose, A
Thy mis - sion is to lead the soul To ho - liest life and love, When
a safe re - pose,
to life and love,

Cov - e - nant — a guid - ing star That no hor - i - zon knows.
earth shall fail to sat - is - fy, Thy gifts the balm shall prove.

My Home.

"Lord, I have loved the habitation of thy house, and the place where thine honor dwelleth."—Psa. xxvi: 8.

Canterbury, N. H.

1. Bright e - ly - sian fields of truth! Gar - dens of God's gifts di - vine!
2. In green pas - tures gen - tly led, By still wa - ters oft I sing,

Foun - tains of His bound - less love! Here's my home for - ev - er.
Par - a - dise of count - less worth, Here's my home for - ev - er.

Sa - cred home! all oth - er climes Pale be - fore thy won - drous light.
Hal - lowed peace! all else be - side Fades be - fore my spir - it's sight.

These will change as works of time,— Thou wilt fail me nev - er.
Mine thro' chang - ing scenes of time, Thou wilt fail me nev - er.

150

Exaltation.

"Give unto the Lord the glory due unto his name."— Psa. xxix : 2.

Canterbury, N. H.

Let the God of my sal-va-tion be ex-alt-ed, Let the God of my sal-va-tion be ex-

alt - ed. Great de-liv-'rance giv-eth He and show - eth mer - cy. For

who is God save the Lord, or who is a rock, is a rock, save our God?

Thou hast giv-en me the shield of Thy sal-va-tion, Thy right hand hath

hold-en me up; Thy gen-tle-ness hath made me great, hath made me great.

It is the Lord that gird-eth me with strength and mak-eth my way,

mak-eth my way per-fect. The Lord . . liv-eth and bless-ed be my rock.

Let the God of my sal-va-tion be ex-alt - - ed, be ex-alt - - - ed.

Canterbury, N. H.

Just e-nough cross by the way, To an-chor the soul in the light,

Just e-nough work by the day, To lead us from er - ror to right.

Just e-nough mer - cy for you, And just e-nough bless-ing for me,

Just e-nough truth to ce - ment, And make us all hap-py and free.

Where I Trust.

"The Eternal God is thy refuge; and underneath are the everlasting arms."— Deut. xxxiii: 27.

Canterbury, N. H.

1. Where - so - e'er the Spir - it call - eth, Let me go, let me go, For as
2. Where - so - e'er the Spir - it call - eth, Let me go, let me go; To em -

not a spar - row fall - eth To the ground but He shall know,
pow - er me for du - ty E'en the heav - ens o - ver - flow.

I will trust no earth - ly bear - ing, I will fear no loss nor
Trust - ful, soul - ful con - se - cra - tion Shall be mine in storm or

harm, Since be - neath the hea - vy bur - den Lies the Ev - er - last - ing
calm, Since be - neath the hea - vy bur - den Lies the Ev - er - last - ing

Arm, Since be - neath the hea - vy bur - den Lies the Ev - er - last - ing Arm.

Holy City.

" I will write upon him the name of my God, and the name of the city of my God,
which is New Jerusalem." — Rev. iii : 12.

Canterbury, N. H.

Ye shall reach the ho - ly cit - y, Ye shall walk its streets of

gold ; All its el - e - ments of beau - ty To thy vis - ion shall un - fold.

When the love of truth shall an - chor Thy whole life in deeds of

light, Pearl - y gates of peace shall o - pen In - to courts for - ev - er bright.

The Beacon.

"To open their eyes, and to turn them from darkness to light."— Acts xxvi: 18

Canterbury, N. H.

1. Far out up-on life's o-cean We see the com-ing sail. The
2. Hold out the bea-con clear - ly, Sal - va - tion's glo-rious ray ; Not
3. In vain we cry the bless-ing Still wait-ing on the shore; A-

waves are in com-mo - tion As old tra-di-tions fail. Sail
in the past, nor fu - ture, We see its light to - day. Let
wake to ac - tive ser - vice, And ply the la - b'ring oar. The

on, brave Ship of Prog - ress, Con - tend with craft and
pres - ent rev - e - la - tion Light up the dark - some
na - tions thirst for know - ledge,—Where is the Sav - iour

creed Un - til the suf - f'ring mil - lions By light and truth are freed.
tide, Un - til our need - y com - rades In har - bor safe - ly ride.
found ? Let vir - gins sing the ad - vent With no un - cer - tain sound.

Hour of Worship.

Worship the Lord in the beauty of holiness.''—1 Chron. xvi : 29.

Canterbury, N. H.

1. O sa - cred hour of wor - ship, When an - gels gath - er nigh With
2. 'Tis heav'n to know my spir - it Is blend - ing with the pure, That

heav'n - ly in - spi - ra - tion To raise our thoughts on high! In
I am stor - ing treas - ures E - ter - nal - ly se - cure; And

faith I of - fer pledg - es Be - fore my Fa - ther's throne, Which
thus I feel ex - alt - ed, Yet hum - ble, when I see How

will re - deem from er - ror And draw His bless - ing down.
good in all His deal - ings My God has been to me.

God is the Lord.

"Blessed art thou, O Lord: teach me thy statutes."— Psa. cxix: 12.

Canterbury, N. H.

God is the Lord, God is the Lord which hath showed us light, hath showed us light.

He is my strength, my strength and my song, He is my strength and my song.

His word have I hid in my heart, His judgments have I laid be -

fore me. I have cho-sen the way of truth. Give me un-der-stand-ing and

I shall keep Thy law, Yea, I will ob-serve it with my whole heart.

I will ob-serve it with my whole heart. I will de-light my-self in

I will ob - serve it with my whole heart.

Thy com-mand-ments, I will de - light my-self in Thy com-mand-ments which

I have loved. O - pen to me the gates of right - eous - ness and

I will go in - to them, and I will go in - to them and

praise the Lord, and praise the Lord, will praise the Lord for - ev - er.

Prayer.

"The Lord heareth the prayer of the righteous."—Prov. xv : 29.

Canterbury, N. H.

1. O Fa - ther, to Thy throne we come In at - ti - tude of prayer, Our
2. O bless us with a fer - vent zeal, To know and do Thy will; With

hearts pe - ti - tion - ing Thy grace, Thy guid - ance, love, and care.
more a - bun - dant right - eous - ness Our un - der - stand - ings fill,

We ask for pow - er to con - trol The el - e - ments of
That we may walk with pur - pose fix'd The path - way of the

earth, For wis - dom, to ex - pand the soul Un - to the high - er birth.
pure, Ful - fill - ing all the law of grace, Thy fa - vor to in - sure.

Willing Service.

"Casting all your care upon him; for he careth for you."—1 Peter v: 7.

Canterbury, N. H.

1. In Thy wis - dom, Fa - ther, guide me In the way that seem - eth
2. When al - lur - ing paths have o - pened To be - guile the way - ward

best; Where-so - e'er I'm need - ed, choose me, To Thy good-ness I'll at - test. In the
step, Thou hast in Thy lov - ing kind - ness An-gels sent to in - ter-cept. Hav-ing

bright - est, dark - est hour Thou hast not for - sak - en me, For be -
guid - ed thus far safe - ly, Led me o - ver dang'rous ways, Rec - og -

yond the gloom has ris - en Just suf - fi - cient light to see.
niz - ing Thy sure mer - cies, I would serve Thee all my days.

Behold, I Stand at the Door.

"I am the good Shepherd, and know my sheep, and am known of mine."—St. John x : 14.

Canterbury, N. H.

Be-hold, I stand at the door and knock: Be-hold, I stand at the

door and knock, I stand at the door and knock. If an - y man hear My

voice and o - pen the door I will come in. Be-hold, I stand and knock, Be -

Be-hold, I stand and

hold, I stand and knock, Be - hold, be - hold I stand, I stand and knock.

knock, Be - hold, I stand and knock,

If an - y man hear my voice, I will come in and sup with him.

Take My yoke up-on you and learn of Me, For I am.

I am meek and meek and low - ly of

heart, and ye shall find rest un - to . . your souls; Take My yoke up - on you and

learn of Me, For I . . am meek and low -ly of heart, and ye shall find rest.

souls, ...

rit.

ye shall find rest un - to your souls, un - to your souls, find rest, find rest.

souls, ...

Going Home.

"Ye ought rather to forgive him, and comfort him, lest perhaps such a one should be swallowed up with overmuch sorrow."—2 Cor. ii: 7.

Canterbury, N. H.

1. I will rise and go to my Fa-ther's house Where bread and wine are free, Where I know the gifts that my spir-it craves Are kind-ly spread for me. I will seek the balm for ev-er-y wound,—For-give-ness, God's pure love; I will take the cross, the bur-den bear, And with the faith-ful move.

2. I . . seek a rest, a . . strength of soul, Found not in sin's do-main,—My right-ful place, an heir-ship true, My Fa-ther's ho-ly name. O . . gift of gifts, for-ev-er mine—Re-demption, full and sure! At . con-se-cra-tion's shrine I bow, My birth-right to se-cure.

164

Appeal.

"He that hath ears to hear, let him hear." — Luke viii: 8.

Canterbury, N. H.

1. Lis - ten, O my Sav-iour, while I come near to pray, And ask rec - og-
2. Hear me, O my Sav-iour, for I seek Thy em - ploy; Earth's best holds no

ni - tion of Thee; Hast Thou not a mes-sage for the strong or the weak, Which
mag - net for me. Lead me to the path-way where the hum - ble are found, Here

Thou canst send trusting-ly by me ? Send me from the self - ish, the world-ly life with-
let me sow pa-tient - ly for Thee. Not in gild-ed pal - ace Thy min - is-try is

in To fields where the seed must be sown; There let me wa - ter and
known, Thy chal - ice of ser - vice I love; Mine be the pow'r of the

work in good faith Till a har - vest for Thee has been grown.
low - ly in heart Ev - 'ry prompt - ing of Thine to ap - prove.

Full Victory.

"Thanks be to God, which giveth us the victory." — 1 Cor. xv: 57.

Canterbury, N. H.

Who mak - eth the des - ert to smile, The waste pla - ces bloom as the

rose, Will sor - row and bur - den be - guile, His arm as a shield in - ter - pose.

I'll pa - tient - ly pass through the flood That na - ture may full vic - t'ry

meet; My Teach - er, my Sav - iour, my God, I find at the blest mer - cy - seat.

Best Gifts.

"They that turn many to righteousness shall shine as the stars for ever and ever."—Dan. xii: 3.

Canterbury, N. H.

Fair - er than ru - bies and rich - er than gold, Are the gems of Christ's

king-dom I see; Wis - dom for ser - vice and pow'r to up - hold Are

gifts most at - trac - tive to me. Clothe and be - deck me with

beau - ty and grace To win pre-cious souls to God's way; To lead in the

light of His glo - ri - ous face, His will all my life shall bear sway.

Peace.

"And the peace of God, which passeth all understanding, shall keep your hearts."—Phil. iv: 7.

Canterbury, N. H.

There's a peace that sur-pass-eth un-der-stand - ing, And joys that the pure in heart do know. Who have followed Christ their Sav - iour O-ver moun-tain and thro' val - ley low. O lead us still on, bless - ed Sav - iour, Till the world we have whol-ly o - ver-come, And we meet with Thee in glo - ry And hear the joy-ful words, "Well done."

Hymn of Praise.

"I will praise thee, O Lord my God, with all my heart; and I will glorify thy name forevermore."— Psa. lxxxvi: 12.

Canterbury, N. H.

I will praise Thee, I will praise Thee, I will praise Thee with my whole heart.

O Lord, with my whole heart.

I will show forth all Thy mar-vellous works, I will be glad and re-

joice in Thee, for Thou hast dealt boun-ti-ful-ly with me. All the

paths of the Lord are mer-cy and truth un-to such as keep His cov-e-nant. The

Lord is nigh un-to all that call up-on Him, and His

law is my de - light. With my whole heart will I praise Thee and will

sing praise un - to Thy name. The right-eous shall give thanks un - to

Thy name, The up - right shall dwell in Thy pres - ence, O Thou Most High.

Canterbury, N. H.

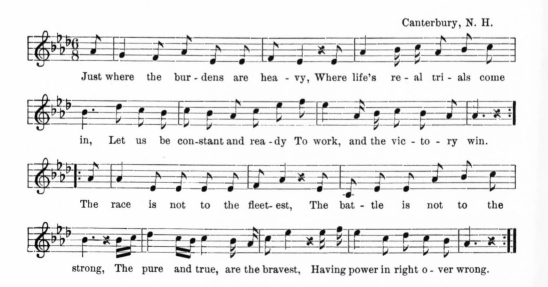

Just where the bur - dens are hea - vy, Where life's re - al tri - als come

in, Let us be con-stant and rea - dy To work, and the vic - to - ry win.

The race is not to the fleet- est, The bat - tle is not to the

strong, The pure and true, are the bravest, Having power in right o - ver wrong.

Endless Growth.

"Grow in grace and in the knowledge of our Lord and Saviour Jesus Christ." — 2 Pet. iii: 18.

Canterbury, N. H.

1. Ev - er chang - ing, ev - er aim - ing Toward a high - er, bet - ter life; Ev - er learn - ing, ev - er earn - ing, Is the per - fect Chris-tian strife. Light un - fold - ing, spir - it mould - ing, Is the law of end - less growth; Feed-ing tho't and word and ac - tion From the wells of bound-less truth.

2. Oft re - view - ing and re - new - ing Con - se - cra - tions made to God, Oft re - pent - ing, ne'er re - sent - ing, At the test - ing of His rod; Mount-ing high - er, draw-ing nigh - er, To the realms of truth and love, Trac- ing du - ty, see-ing beau - ty In the laws He doth ap - prove.

3. Be it ev - er our en - deav - or As the sand our time-glass fills, To be mould - ed by the Pot - ter, In the fash - ion that He wills; For He know - eth and He do - eth What - so - e'er is wise and just. Let us all, with hum-ble spir - it, In His keep - ing place our trust.

The Overcomer.

"He that hath an ear, let him hear what the Spirit saith."— Rev. ii: 7.

1. To him that o-ver-com-eth will I grant to sit with me; I share My Fa-ther's
2. To him that o-ver-com-eth o-pen wide the ci-ty gates; No night is there, no

king-dom, there al-so he shall be. No harm shall o-ver-take him who
sor-row,heav'n's golden morn-ing waits; No more the roll-ing sea surf, no

work-eth to the end, But pow-er o-ver na-tions up-on him shall descend. A
sin can en-ter there, But joys in life e-ter-nal,tran-scend-ing earth-ly care. The

pil-lar in God's tem-ple, who o-ver-comes I'll make, Go no more out for-
Lamb of God shall lead him where liv-ing wa-ters flow, The tree of life shall

ev-er; a new name shall he take, He'll feed on hid-den man-na, Be
feed him, bless-ed peace shall he know. Like voice of ma-ny wa-ters My

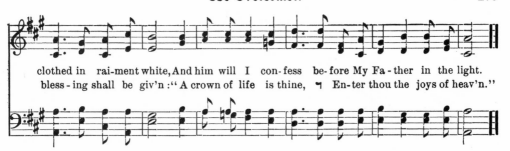

clothed in rai-ment white, And him will I con-fess be-fore My Fa-ther in the light.
bless-ing shall be giv'n :" A crown of life is thine, ¬ En-ter thou the joys of heav'n."

Thanksgiving.

"He hath called you out of darkness into his marvellous light."—1 Peter ii: 9.

Canterbury, N. H.

Break forth, O my soul, In songs of thanks-giv-ing, Ren-der a

trib-ute To the God of the liv-ing. For He hath called thee,

Called thee from dark-ness; Sing of His bound-less love With joy and glad-ness.

Continuing City.

"Here have we no continuing city, but we seek one to come."— Heb. xiii: 14.

Canterbury, N. H.

Here I've no con - tin-uing cit - y, But I'm seek - ing one to come; In the

house of man - y man - sions Is my ev - er - last - ing home, In the

house of man - y man - sions Is my ev - er - last - ing home. As I'm

ris - ing high - er, high - er, Near - er to the light each day, Ho - ly

each day,

an - gels bring me tid - ings From my home not far a - way, From my

home not far a - way, not far a - way. 2. Here I'm giv - ing Chris-tian

ser - vice As I'm work - ing heart and hand, Here I'm learn - ing need-ful

les - sons, Fit -ting for the Bet - ter Land. Far a - bove all mists and

shad - ows I can see the gold - en dawn, I can hear the voice of

loved ones From my ev - er - last - ing home, from my ev - er - last - ing home.

The Journey Heavenward.

"Ye shall go out with joy, and be led forth with peace." — Isa. lv: 12.

Canterbury, N. H.

All the way shin-eth brighter as near-er I come To the king-dom of

light, peace and love; And the cross bring-eth bless-ing when hum-bly I

seek For the rich-es of heav-en a-bove. I would know Thy sal-va-tion and

learn of the truth That from all earth-ly ties will re-deem; O guide me for-

ev-er be-side wa-ters pure, Let me drink of the clear heal-ing stream.

God be Praised.

"If I forget thee, O Jerusalem, let my right hand forget her cunning; let my tongue cleave to the roof of my mouth if I prefer not Jerusalem above my chief joy."—Psa. cxxxvii: 6.

Canterbury, N. H.

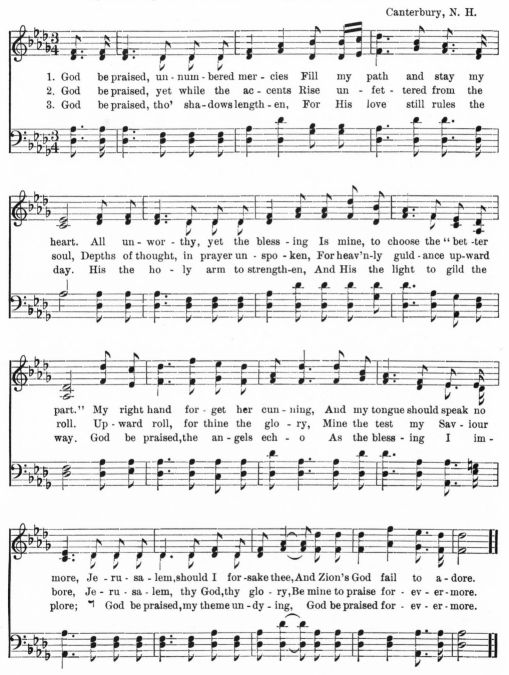

1. God be praised, un-num-bered mer-cies Fill my path and stay my
2. God be praised, yet while the ac-cents Rise un-fet-tered from the
3. God be praised, tho' sha-dows length-en, For His love still rules the

heart. All un-wor-thy, yet the bless-ing Is mine, to choose the "bet-ter
soul, Depths of thought, in prayer un-spo-ken, For heav'n-ly guid-ance up-ward
day. His the ho-ly arm to strength-en, And His the light to gild the

part." My right hand for-get her cun-ning, And my tongue should speak no
roll. Up-ward roll, for thine the glo-ry, Mine the test my Sav-iour
way. God be praised, the an-gels ech-o As the bless-ing I im-

more, Je-ru-sa-lem, should I for-sake thee, And Zion's God fail to a-dore.
bore, Je-ru-sa-lem, thy God, thy glo-ry, Be mine to praise for-ev-er-more.
plore; ¶ God be praised, my theme un-dy-ing, God be praised for-ev-er-more.

178

Thy Treasure.

"For where your treasure is, there will your heart be also."— Matt. vi: 21.

Canterbury, N. H.

1. Peace di - vine, in - creas - ing meas - ure, Joy and tri - umph thou shalt
2. Peace with God, the soul at - tain - ment Of a heart at one with

find In the life of Christ thy treas - ure, Sa - cred trust and truth com -
Him, Peace on earth, good-will a - bid - eth Where the Christ hath en - tered

bined. Here may all by wise en - deav - or Hold in faith the gos - pel
in. Like thy Sav - iour, bear good tid - ings, Her - ald peace o'er earth and

key, For where the treas - ure, Christ hath said, Thy heart will al - so
sea, For where the treas - ure, Christ hath said, Thy heart will al - so

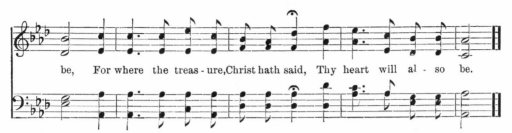

be,   For where the treas - ure, Christ hath said, Thy heart will al - so be.

𝕿𝖍𝖊 𝕾𝖕𝖎𝖗𝖎𝖙'𝖘 𝕸𝖊𝖘𝖘𝖆𝖌𝖊.

"They shall not prevail against thee ; for I am with thee, saith the Lord."—Jer. i: 19.

Canterbury, N. H.

What does the Spir - it whis - per, What mes - sage to us   con - vey? Be

loy - al in faith and prin - ci - ple, Let Truth her scep - ter sway.

Self - ish at - trac - tions may call thee, The world with its fol - lies as -

sail, But God in His love will strengthen, Fear not, thou shalt pre - vail.

Blest Retreat.

"Learn of me ; for I am meek and lowly in heart : and ye shall find rest unto your souls."—Matt. xi : 29.

Canterbury, N. H.

1. In - to the sa - cred, blest re - treat Of low - li - ness and prayer, Oft
2. Pray'r o - pens wide the pearl - y gates Of low - li - ness and peace ; O

let us turn our way - ward feet, And find a sol - ace there.
en - ter where the har - vest waits, To bless with its in - crease.

There lis - ten to the still small voice Of con-science, while it pleads For
May watch - ful-ness and pray'r com-bined, Their time - ly vig - ils keep, And

each to live to high - est light, As day to day suc - ceeds.
lov - ing deeds, with words re - fined, Be ours to sow and reap.

Hidden Riches.

"I will give thee the treasures of darkness, and hidden riches of secret places."— Isa. xlv: 3.

Canterbury, N. H.

1. O climb a steep-er height And breathe a pur-er air, Take
2. Seek thou be-neath the sur-face And find the pearls of truth, The

vis-ion of the land be-yond, Thy heav'n-ly king-dom fair. Thou'lt
rich-es of the heav-ens fair Can ne'er com-pare with earth. Who

reach its flow-'ry bor-ders, Thou'lt find its prom-ised peace, As
finds the hid-den man-na Will speak the lan-guage new, Who

earth with all its tur-moil Shall in thy pre-cincts cease.
serves the Lord with mind and strength Hath found the king-dom true.

What Shall It Avail?

"What shall it profit a man, if he shall gain the whole world, and lose his own soul?"— Mark viii: 36.

Canterbury, N. H.

1. What shall it a - vail, when time is no more, That I've gar- nered rich
2. What shall it a - vail, in E - ter - ni - ty's day, That earth's night was

treas - ures of vain earth - ly lore? O what shall it a - vail, when the
gild - ed with pleas - ure's bright sway? In bal - ance di - vine on - ly

reap - ers shall say, "Not this and not that can ye take on your way?"
Christ-hood is weight, Self - con - quest the pass at the strait, nar -row gate.

What shall it a - vail? O what shall it a - vail? The rich - es of
What shall it a - vail At ebb of the tide My strength here was

earth—must they ut - ter - ly fail?"Dust to dust," is the an-swer,"on - ly
giv'n with Christ to a - bide? All, all shall it a - vail; The

spir - it will last; O here lay thy treas-ure, thy an - chor make fast."
first- fruits I bring, The full - ness of life to my Sav - iour, my King.

Promise.

"The Lord shall arise upon thee, and his glory shall be seen upon thee."— Isa. lx: 2.

Canterbury, N. H.

O Zi - on, be law - a - bid - ing, In the love of truth con- fid - ing,

Tho' my face may séem as hid - ing And thy en - e - mies bear sway.

I will rise in thee, a tower Strong in light and end - less power;

And thy dark or shad - ed hour Shall break be - fore re - splend- ent day.

Gift of God.

"The water that I shall give him shall be in him a well of water springing up into everlasting life." — St. John iv: 14.

Canterbury, N. H.

1. Give me to drink, I pray Thee, Lord, Thy wells are run-ning
2. Give me to drink, I ask in faith, O Lord, Thou canst be-

o'er; O grant the gift of God to me, And I shall thirst no
stow; From foun-tains of Thy rich-est grace E-ter-nal bless-ings

more, O I shall thirst no more. I need not search the
flow, E-ter-nal bless-ings flow. The need-y soul no

hid-den depths, Nor climb the moun-tain high, Thy gift, O God, is
more shall thirst, Who liv-ing streams hath sought; Since Christ is King, the

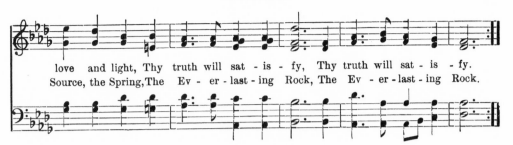

love and light, Thy truth will sat - is - fy, Thy truth will sat - is - fy.
Source, the Spring, The Ev - er - last - ing Rock, The Ev - er - last - ing Rock.

Guiding Star.

"According to your faith be it unto you."— Matt. ix : 29.

Canterbury, N. H.

Seems the reap - er yet to lin - ger? Seems the har - vest yet a - far?

Grow not hope - less, bear on ev - er, Faith is life's bright guid - ing star.

Guid - ing star to truth e - ter - nal, Where earth's tur-moils have no sway;

Where the soul in con-scious vic - t'ry Knows one long and hap - py day.

At One with Christ.

"Learn of me; for I am meek and lowly in heart: and ye shall find rest unto your souls." — Matt. xi: 29.

Canterbury, N. H.

1. Wouldst thou crown thy life with glo - ry? Wouldst thou hal-low ev - 'ry deed? Seek the
2. Wouldst thou catch a glimpse of heav - en? Where the pure in heart a-bide? Wouldst thou

love of Christ, the Sav - iour As the balm for ev - 'ry need. What the
hold thy trust se - cure - ly Thro' the ebb and flow of tide? Fix thy

bur - den of thy sor - row? Why the tur - moil of thy soul? Live for
heart on joys im - mor - tal, Lay thy treas - ure e'en so high That the

Zi - on's pur - est in - t'rest, Let her needs thy pow'r con - trol.
mists of earth - ly form - ing Can - not dim or cloud thy sky.

Here Am I.

"Here am I; for thou didst call me." — 1 Sam. iii : 8.

Canterbury, N. H.

1. O Fa - ther, with the sig - net Of Thy un - dy - ing love For -
2. Wouldst Thou di - rect me thith - er O'er yon tem - pest - uous flood, My
3. Speak, Lord, Thy ser - vant hear - eth, And glad - ly will o - bey; What -

ev - er seal my spir - it, That I Thine own may prove.
faith in Thee is an - chored, Thou know - est my best good.
e'er Thou wouldst, my Fa - ther, Make known to me, I pray.

Teach me to know Thy voice, Though tem - pests may de - fy;
And when I hear Thy call O may I e'er re - ply
What - ev - er cares op - press, What - ev - er in - t'rests try,

Let me be clothed with grace To an - swer, "Here am I."
With true sub - mis - sive heart, My Fa - ther, "Here am I."
I'll trust my all with Thee And an - swer, "Here am I."

Revelation.

"Other foundation can no man lay than that is laid, which is Jesus Christ."—1 Cor. iii: 11.

Canterbury, N. H.

1. O build as the wise build, on the Rock of A - ges, By true rev - e -
2. O build as the wise build, with un - err - ing pur - pose, O build toward the

la - tion the Pat - tern we know; O build with the knowledge that " hay, wood, and
i - deals of e - ter - nal right; O build, and thy tem - ple so strong and en -

stub - ble " En - dure not the fur - nace nor strong winds that blow. The
dur - ing Shall rise to per - fec - tion in man - sions of light. Kind

sand and the quick-sand, the self - ish and world - ly, All fail by the
deeds to " the least " are the stones for thy build - ing, O seal them with

test - ing of truth and its light, But Christ, our Foun - da - tion, our
love, this the flood - tide de - fies; Not made with the hands is the

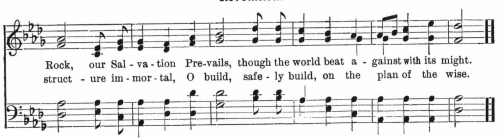

Rock, our Sal-va-tion Pre-vails, though the world beat a-gainst with its might.
struct-ure im-mor-tal, O build, safe-ly build, on the plan of the wise.

Blessing.

"It is more blessed to give than to receive." — Acts xx : 35.

Canterbury, N. H.

When I seek di-vine ac-cept-ance, Or im-plore God's bless-ing

pure, Comes the an-swer : "Bless each oth-er, This will heav-en's best se-cure.

Ye have Christ, a liv-ing Sav-iour, The Mil-len-ni-um be-

gun, When to oth-ers ye are faith-ful As ye ask their du-ties done."

The Landing.

"These are they which came out of great tribulation."— Rev. vii: 14.

Canterbury, N. H.

1. I shall meet the brave souls at the Land - ing, When shore un - to shore
2. I shall sing with the hosts at the Land - ing, The song of re - demp -

shall re - spond; Where kin - dred and guard-ians are joy - ful To
tion and grace, For "deep un - to deep" giv - eth an - swer As

wid - en the spir - it - ual bond. I shall meet them as friends of the
lines of re - mem-brance we trace. At the Land- ing, the theme of sal -

Sav - iour, Who vic - t'ry in earth - life have found; Where he
va - tion Shall swell in an un - bro - ken chord; Bless - ed

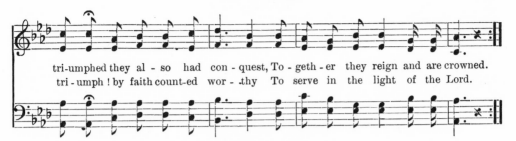

tri-umphed they al - so had con-quest, To-geth-er they reign and are crowned.
tri-umph! by faith count-ed wor-thy To serve in the light of the Lord.

Unclouded Day.

"But the path of the just is as the shining light, that shineth more and more unto the perfect day."—
Prov. iv: 18.

Canterbury, N. H.

The sun and stars may roll their way, Withhold or give their shin - ing. My

soul hath light in end - less day That needs no sil - ver lin - ing. No

earth - ly clouds of strife are there, For faith and trust have con - quered ; And

all who may this bless - ing share In truth and love are an - chored.

Security.

"Lay not up for yourselves treasures upon earth."—Matt. vi: 19.

Canterbury, N. H.

1. Not be - low the clouds be build - ing, Blight-ing frosts there hold their
2. Far a - bove the clouds thy heav - en Spans the blue, re - veals the

sway ; Nor with earth-ly hopes be gild- ing Home and treas-ure for thy stay.
gold, Pearls of last - ing lus - ter, hid -den In the depths of love un - told.

God has called thee to in - her - it Rich - es of im - mor - tal
Gains and gifts that know no blight - ing Hold thy heart in pur - pose

worth ; Give thy heart un - to the spir - it, While thy la - bor is on earth.
pure, Earth and heav-en thus u - nit-ing, Home and her - i - tage se - cure.

Hallowed.

"Thy will be done in earth, as it is in heaven." — Matt. vi ; 10.

Canterbury, N. H.

1. Let me dwell in bliss - ful man - sions, Though I move 'mid scenes be - low;
2. Heav'n - ly mis - sion, Christ - like ser - vice, Is my rest, my strength, my praise;

Let the spir - it guide and fash - ion Ev - 'ry mo - tive, as I go.
Here in will - ing con - se - cra - tion Let me of - fer all my days.

Thus I have di - vine as - sur - ance — Ne'er can mur - mur at my lot —
Ho - ly treas - ures to my keep - ing Give the pow'rs that test and prove,

Heav - en here and heav'n here - aft - er Makes of home a hal - lowed spot.
Peace that pass - eth un - der - stand - ing, Wis - dom wrought in God a - bove.

The New Language.

"Then will I turn to the people a pure language."—Zeph. iii: 9.

Canterbury, N. H.

1. O give me lan-guage whol-ly pure, Or words which may no
2. O give me lan-guage whol-ly wise, From heart at rest with

soul of-fend, And let my voice the weak as-sure The
gos-pel sight, Let words of com-fort up-ward rise As

cross hath bless-ings with-out end. I've felt its power as one a-lone, Its
mu-sic toward the God of light. In-spire my lips to voice Thy word, Con-

worth when with com-pan-ions blest; Of all the gifts God's love hath strown,The
vic-tion of Thy love su-preme; The el-o-quence by heav-en stirred Hath

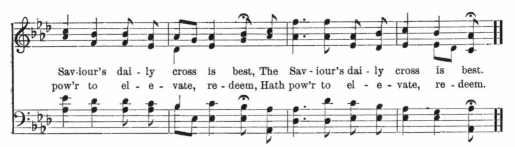

Sav-iour's dai - ly cross is best, The Sav - iour's dai - ly cross is best.
pow'r to el - e - vate, re - deem, Hath pow'r to el - e - vate, re - deem.

God's Care.

"I have loved thee with an everlasting love; therefore with loving kindness have I drawn thee."—
Jer. xxxi: 3.

Canterbury, N. H.

How can I for a mo - ment For - get God's ten - der care? How

can I e'en in sor - row For - get the love I share?

For - bid it, O my Sav - iour, That doubt or fear pre - vail, I

rest with - in thy judg - ment Where mer - cy can - not fail.

Star of Purity.

"Blessed are the pure in heart; for they shall see God."—Matt. v: 8.

Canterbury, N. H.

1. O bright - er than the morn - ing star Is the heart that's pure and
2. The gems with - in the o - cean deep, And the wealth her cav - erns

free; And the light that's ev - er glow - ing there,—The Star of Pu - ri - ty.
bear, Let the o - cean and her cav - erns keep, In dark-ness hid - den there.

The sun shall wane, the stars go down, And reign of time be o'er; But the
But O, al-might - y Fa - ther, send Thine an - gels from a - bove, To

liv - ing light in the heart that's pure Shall shine for - ev - er more.
kin - dle in . . my heart a fire Of pu - ri - ty and love.

In Thy Name.

"The barrel of meal wasted not, neither did the cruse of oil fail, according to the word of the Lord."—1 Kings xvii: 16.

Canterbury, N. H.

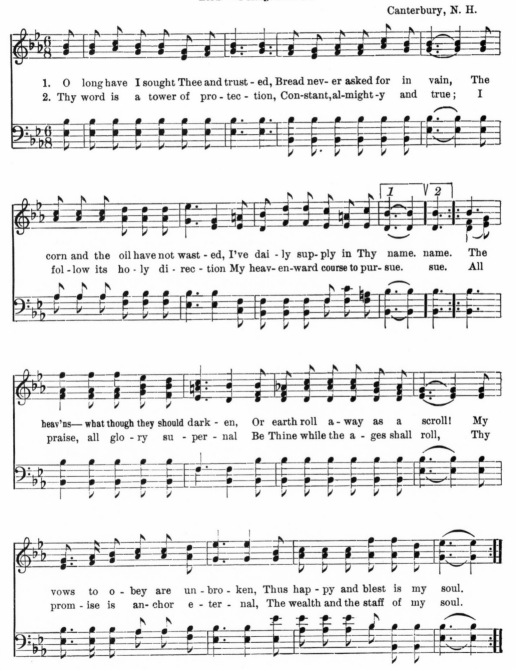

1. O long have I sought Thee and trust-ed, Bread nev-er asked for in vain, The
2. Thy word is a tower of pro-tec-tion, Con-stant, al-might-y and true; I

corn and the oil have not wast-ed, I've dai-ly sup-ply in Thy name. name. The
fol-low its ho-ly di-rec-tion My heav-en-ward course to pur-sue. sue. All

heav'ns— what though they should dark-en, Or earth roll a-way as a scroll! My
praise, all glo-ry su-per-nal Be Thine while the a-ges shall roll, Thy

vows to o-bey are un-bro-ken, Thus hap-py and blest is my soul.
prom-ise is an-chor e-ter-nal, The wealth and the staff of my soul.

Chosen.

"I have chosen you out of the world." — St. John xv : 19.

Canterbury, N. H.

I walk thro' the val - ley and meet God there, I rise to the moun - tain still

feel - ing His care; A - mid throng or des - ert thrill - ing whis - pers de - clare, —

"I have cho - sen thee, come fol - low me; I have cho - sen thee, come fol - low me."

Fol - low Thee? fol - low Thee? My whole soul re - plies, I grasp the hand out -

stretched and stand with the wise, with the wise. Tho' calm may suc - ceed, tho'

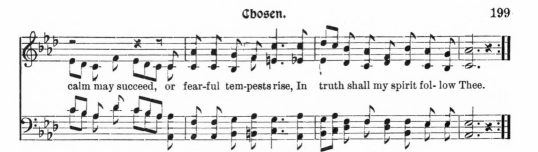

calm may succeed, or fear-ful tem-pests rise, In truth shall my spirit fol- low Thee.

Life Triumphant.

"O death, where is thy sting? O grave, where is thy victory?"—1 Cor. xv: 55.

Canterbury, N. H.

1. Be-yond all earth-ly sor-row, Be-yond earth's self-ish claim, I've
2. With love I fill my meas-ure And grate-ful trib-ute bring, Pos -

found a glad to-mor-row And joy-ful-ly ex-claim, "O
sess the good-ly treas-ure, And with the ran-somed sing, O

grave, where is thy vic-to-ry? O death, where is thy sting? O
O grave, where is thy vic-to-ry? O death, where is thy sting?

Repeat Cho. pp after last verse.

grave, where is thy vic-to-ry? O death, where is thy sting?"

Christian Ministry.

"And Jesus said unto them, They need not depart; give ye them to eat." — Matt. xiv: 16.

Canterbury, N. H.

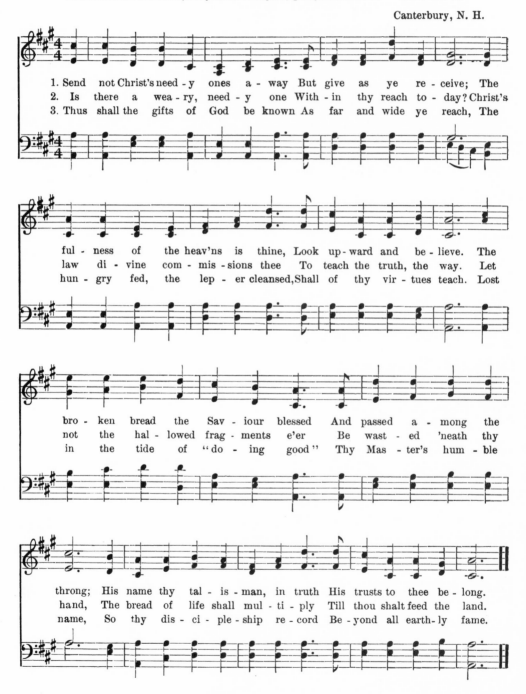

1. Send not Christ's need-y ones a-way But give as ye re-ceive; The
ful-ness of the heav'ns is thine, Look up-ward and be-lieve. The
bro-ken bread the Sav-iour blessed And passed a-mong the
throng; His name thy tal-is-man, in truth His trusts to thee be-long.

2. Is there a wea-ry, need-y one With-in thy reach to-day? Christ's
law di-vine com-mis-sions thee To teach the truth, the way. Let
not the hal-lowed frag-ments e'er Be wast-ed 'neath thy
hand, The bread of life shall mul-ti-ply Till thou shalt feed the land.

3. Thus shall the gifts of God be known As far and wide ye reach, The
hun-gry fed, the lep-er cleansed, Shall of thy vir-tues teach. Lost
in the tide of "do-ing good" Thy Mas-ter's hum-ble
name, So thy dis-ci-ple-ship re-cord Be-yond all earth-ly fame.

Chief Delight.

"The grass withereth, the flower fadeth : but the word of our God shall stand forever."—Isa. xl: 8.

Canterbury, N. H.

1. When the lil - ies fade a - way, Gold as dust hath found its place,
2. When the ros - es' bloom is gone, When the gems of earth are riven,

Still my joys and com - forts stay,— Fruits of hum - ble, trust - ing grace.
Still my con - fi - dence, my home, Rest in last - ing joys of heav'n.

In the gar - den of God's love Blooms the Ev - er - last - ing Right;
In the boun - ty of God's care, No dis - may my trust can blight;

In its law, from truth a - bove, Hath my soul its chief de - light;
Here in wealth be - yond com - pare, Hath my soul its chief de - light;

In its law, from truth a - bove, Hath my soul its chief de - light.
Here in wealth be - yond com - pare, Hath my soul its chief de - light.

In Christ's Name.

"Seek ye first the kingdom of God and his righteousness."— Matt. vi: 33.

Canterbury, N. H.

1. Have ye asked in Christ's name, That a bless- ing from heav'n May hal - low each
2. Have ye served in Christ's name? With the need- y oft prayed That the light of His

aim, As Thy ser - vice is given? Are ye seek - ing the king-dom As first
king-dom O'er the earth may be spread? Are ye sealed as dis - ci - ples By the

in - t'rest and care? Will thy earn -est en - deav - or Se - cure treas - ure there?
love ye be - stow? With the rich -ness of heav - en Doth thy life o - ver -flow?

We have asked in Christ's name, And the bless - ing came near As the ra - diant
We have served in Christ's name, And the bless - ing came near As the ra - diant

sun - shine With its mes - sage to cheer; We have prayed that the

king - dom In true right - eous - ness come, That on earth as in

heav - en God's will may be done, God's will may be done.

True Wealth.

"The depth saith, It is not in me : and the sea saith, It is not with me."— Job xxviii : 14.

Canterbury, N. H.

There's wealth in mines of gold, There's wealth in depths of sea ; But earth, the wealth of

gos - pel love Was nev - er born of thee. A household heav - en-wide, A

par - ent-age in God, Christ's gos-pel does pro - vide For all who keep His word.

What Will Bring the Heavens Nearer?

"When ye see these things come to pass, know ye that the kingdom of God is nigh at hand." — Luke xxi: 31.

Canterbury, N. H.

1. What will bring the heav - ens near-er? Psalms of praise and hymns of prayer;
2. What will bring the heav - ens near-er? Seek - ing first "thy king - dom come,"
3. What will bring the heav - ens near-er? "Love thy neigh - bor as thy-self,"

Not a - lone these rise as sa - vor, To the need - y give thy care." It is
Prayed and prom -ised by the Sav-iour; Lo, with-in its reign shall dawn, Here un-
Love thy en - e - my, and nev -er E - vil give, since good is wealth. Thus My

I" who walk a -mong you Ask - ing bread for life to- day, Who withholds the Christian
fold - ing and re-mold-ing, Leav-'ning ev - 'ry word and deed, Min-is-t'ring a sav-ing
king-dom is es - tab-lished And thy heav - en here be-gun, The new earth shall bloom in

ser - vice Puts God's bless - ing far a - way, Puts God's blessing far a - way.
power, Answ'ring full thine ev - 'ry need, Answ'ring full thine ev - 'ry need.
glad - ness As My will in thine is done, As My will in thine is done.

The New Name.

I will give him a white stone, and in the stone a new name written, which no man knoweth saving he that
receiveth it."— Rev. ii: 17.

Canterbury, N. H.

What will the pas-sage through Jor - dan be, As ye
pass to the Ci - ty of Light, That a pure new name be
given to thee, And thy spir - it be robed in white? Is the
sac - ri - fice wor- thy the bless - ing? Will the cross ex - ceed the crown? Then
of - fer thy meed of re - joic - ing, For the power of the Christ is found.

The Angel's Record.

"Rejoice because your names are written in heaven." — Luke x : 20.

Canterbury, N. H.

1. O write my name in heav'n A - mong the vir - gins pure, O
2. O write my name in heav'n Where moth can nev - er blight; O

write my name in heav'n For I ev - er will en - dure. There's no
lay my treas - ure there Be - yond the shades of night. All

halt - ing, no ex - cus - ing, No turn - ing back for me, For the
hop - ing, all con - fid - ing, My trust is an - chored there, For the

glo - ries, O the glo - ries Of the bet - ter land I see.
rich - es, O the rich - es Of the heav'ns my soul would share.

Confiding.

" Behold, he that keepeth Israel shall neither slumber nor sleep." — Psa. cxxi: 4.

Canterbury, N. H.

1. I know that I ask not in vain Thy bless - ing to hal - low my day, Thy
2. I know that Thy foun - tain of love Will moun-tain and val - ley o'er - flow, Not

spir - it with - in me to reign And teach of Thy glo - ri - fied way.
bar - ren nor thirst - y the soul Who serves where the path - way is low.

I know that Thine eye nev - er sleeps, Thine ear heeds the least of my prayer, Thy
Then on - ward and up - ward my life Shall rise to Thy glo - ry and praise, For

mer - cy a kind vig - il keeps Till bit - ter is sweet 'neath Thy care.
in - to this spir - it - ual strife I en - ter for full - ness of days.

Growth.

"Consider the lilies of the field, how they grow."— Matt. vi: 28.

Canterbury, N. H.

1. As opes the li - ly fair . . To drink the dews of morn, So
2. As grows the li - ly fair . . Be - neath the skies so blue, Ex -

wakes each heart to share The light of heav - en's dawn. With - in its rays so
pand - ing pet - als rare From spot - less heart so true, With ca - lyx of pure

blest, The way is bright and clear; The soul here - in finds rest, Since
gold, Its heart with vir - tue bright, So Chris - tian grace is told By

1 **2**

Christ is ev - er near.
truth's un - sul - lied *(Omit.)* light, . . By truth's un - sul - lied light.

3. No sun, no bril - liant star, Can with this light com - pare; It shines o'er hill - tops
4. No night, no deep - 'ning shade, Can dim this lus - ter fair; Its glo - ry can - not

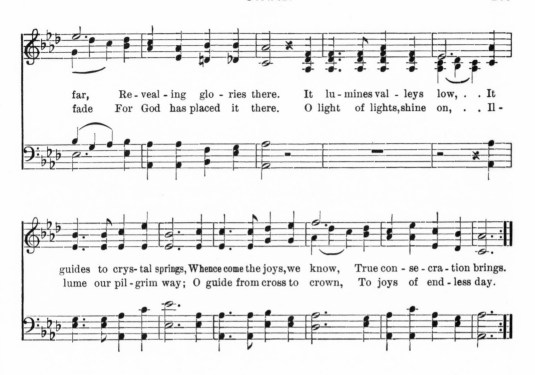

far, Re - veal - ing glo - ries there. It lu - mines val - leys low, . . It
fade For God has placed it there. O light of lights, shine on, . . Il -

guides to crys- tal springs, Whence come the joys, we know, True con - se - cra - tion brings.
lume our pil - grim way; O guide from cross to crown, To joys of end - less day.

Canterbury, N. H.

In whose ser - vice art thou toil - ing? What the ob - ject of thy

care? Will the seed which thou art sow-ing, Bloom in spir - it fruit-age fair?

Will the reap - ing of life's har - vest Yield e - ter - nal life to

thee? O my soul, be wise in sow - ing, That the har - vest blest may be.

Our Mansion.

"We have a building of God, an house not made with hands, eternal in the heavens." — 2 Cor. v: 1.

Canterbury, N. H.

1. While here we are build-ing each day A man-sion here-af-ter our own, We
2. When high-er the frame-work doth rise, A tem-ple of hon-or to be, Im-
3. Then grand-ly our struc-ture shall rise In praise to the Build-er di-vine, Whose

choose neith-er stub-ble nor clay But rocks from God's quar-ry a-lone.
bed-ded in God, the All-Wise, Foun-da-tion the deep-er have we.
good-ness no wis-dom de-nies To fol-low His wondrous de-sign.

Though ce-dar o'er-laid with pure gold Is cost-ly, the price we will pay, For
Here tem-pests may roll on in vain, The spir-it has per-fect con-trol, For
What rich-es e-ter-nal! What peace We find for our store-house so fair! Each

tim-ber the Christ pow'r doth hold Stands sure though the world pass a-way.
e-vil can nev-er re-main When Christ is en-shrined in the soul.
day as these bless-ings in-crease Our souls hum-bly build on in prayer.

Protecting Hand.

"He leadeth me in the paths of righteousness for his name's sake."—Psa. xxiii : 3.

Canterbury, N. H.

God's love to me,

1. I may not reach the height nor depth Of God's great love to me, Nor

whis- per low,

2. I may not catch all coun -sel wise The heav-ens whis-per low, Nor

view the Hand which turned my feet From harm I could not see;
claim the full - ness of their wealth That charms my spir - it so;

But this I know,—I've felt its worth and trust its sav - ing
But this I know,— I here re - ly Where time and tide are

pow'r, I ask this search-ing, guid - ing light In ev - 'ry pass-ing hour.
sav - ing pow'r,
o'er, In God a - lone my trust su-preme Is an-chored ev - er - more.
are o'er,

The Vineyard.

"Go ye also into the vineyard." — Matt. xx : 4.

Canterbury, N. H.

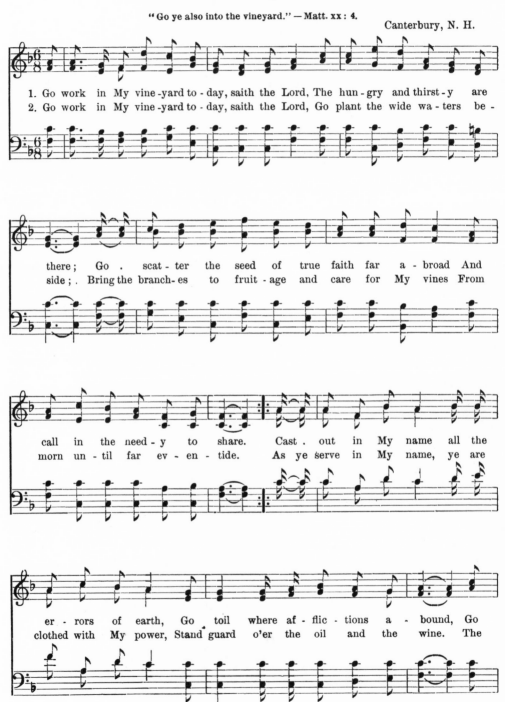

1. Go work in My vine-yard to-day, saith the Lord, The hun-gry and thirst-y are
2. Go work in My vine-yard to-day, saith the Lord, Go plant the wide wa-ters be -

there ; Go . scat-ter the seed of true faith far a-broad And
side ; . Bring the branch-es to fruit-age and care for My vines From

call in the need-y to share. Cast . out in My name all the
morn un-til far ev-en-tide. As ye serve in My name, ye are

er-rors of earth, Go toil where af-flic-tions a-bound, Go
clothed with My power, Stand guard o'er the oil and the wine. The

pub-lish the light which per-fects the new birth, The light a full Sav-iour is found.
vin-tage is full and My prom-ise se- cure; If true, peace and blessing be thine.

Heaven's Highway.

"And an highway shall be there, and a way, and it shall be called The way of holiness." — Isa. xxxv: 8.

Canterbury, N. H.

Lift thine eyes, O Chris-tian pil-grim, Catch the light that gilds the

day, An-gel min-is-ters are call-ing, "Come up high-er, pass this way."

No more fear, no dread nor doubt-ing, Heav-en's high-way's not man-

made; Let its gifts thy soul be light-ing, On its joys thy feet be staid.

Heaven.

"He that overcometh, the same shall be clothed in white raiment."— Rev. iii: 5.

Canterbury, N. H.

1. I shall know My own in heav - en, God's pure chil - dren of the
2. I shall know My own in heav - en, By a new and hal -lowed

light, All their sins have been for - giv - en And their robes are pearl - y white.
name, An - gel min - is - try their glo - ry, Win-ning souls with Christ to reign.

I shall know them in their white - ness, All of self is washed a -
I shall hear their ho - ly voi - ces, I shall see their work di -

way; I shall know them in their brightness, An - gels of e - ter - nal day.
vine Ris - ing un - to heights e - ter - nal; I shall know them—they are Mine.

Resolution.

"They that trust in the Lord shall be as Mount Zion, which cannot be removed, but abideth forever."— Psa. cxxv: 1.

Canterbury, N. H.

I draw no blank nor miss the prize, I see the work, the sac - ri - fice, And with the loy - al I'll be wise, A faith-ful o - ver-com - er.

I am as sure that heav'n is mine As though my vi - sion could de - fine Or pen - cil draw the boun - da - ry line Where love in truth shall con - quer.

Mission of Life.

"I have set the Lord always before me: because he is at my right hand, I shall not be moved." — Psa. xvi: 8.

Enfield, N. H.

I will stand as the oak 'mid the tem - pest and storm, Yet hum - ble in

spir - it would tru - ly be - come, De - vot - ed to Zi - on's whole

in - t'rest and gain, That in her fair courts I may right - ful - ly reign.

O ban - ish all thought of con - ten - tion and strife With God - giv - en

faith in my mis - sion of life; A full con - se - cra - tion hence -

forth shall be mine Of all I pos-sess, in God's ser-vice di-vine.

Fervor.

"He giveth power to the faint; and to them that have no might he increaseth strength."— Isa. xl: 29.

Canterbury, N. H.

I nev-er would wea-ry in watch-ing, Or pray-ing, my Fa-ther, to

Thee; I nev-er would faint in well-do-ing, There-by I come near-er to

Thee. The price of the con-flict I've count-ed; Give all, re-ceive all in

Christ; In no oth-er way is it grant-ed To hold the true rich-es in trust.

The Harvest Home.

"Neither is he that planteth any thing, neither he that watereth; but God that giveth the increase." — 1 Cor. iii: 7.

Canterbury, N. H.

1. The seed-time is past, the har-vest is o'er, The wheat safe-ly gar-nered with care; But what of the yield? Hath full hun-dred-fold Re-ward-ed our la-bors of prayer? O what is the claim in bal-an-ces true, Is it gain or loss that we find? Did we sow in full

2. The har-vest is o'er, the gar-ners are full, With plen-ty the year has been crowned. Our hearts sing in praise to the Lord of the yield, Whose good-ness and mer-cy a-bound. Our trib-ute of joy un-trammelled shall rise, Con-tin-ue, O bless-ing di-vine. We plant for Thy

trust and pa - tient - ly reap   That our will to God's be re - signed?
sake, we reap in Thy name,   The glo - ry of fruit - age is Thine.

Standard-Bearers.

"Lift up a standard for the people."— Isa. lxii: 10.

Canterbury, N. H.

Li - on - heart - ed, brave and true,   God hath not for - got - ten you,

And His arm is sure to do   What His love hath prom - ised.

Stand - ard-bear - ers, for - ward press!   By the light of ho - li - ness.

Ah, no foe, no wil - der - ness Can sep - a - rate you from Him.

Resignation.

"Thou wilt keep him in perfect peace, whose mind is stayed on thee." — Isa. xxvi: 3.

Canterbury, N. H.

1. I may not ask where Thou wouldst lead, It is e-nough to know Thou
2. I may not ask why Thou hast wrought These low-ly tasks for me, Nor

dost my fer-vent prayer heed, De-fine each whis-per low.
why Thy wis-er heart sought My life to hon-or Thee.

I trust Thee, Fa-ther, Moth-er,—God, Thou wilt, as Thou hast done, Re-
I trust Thy guid-ance ev-er-more, Nor mur-mur at Thy voice, In

mem-ber in pa-ren-tal love The daugh-ter and the son.
Thee my con-fi-dence re-store, O make Thy will my choice.

Treasure in Heaven.

"Lay up for yourselves treasures in heaven." — Matt. vi: 20.

Canterbury, N. H.

1. I am lay - ing up my treas - ure Where no moth or rust can
2. As the sow - ing, so the har - vest, Each sea - son in its

blight, Joy and peace will crown my la - bor, As I tri - umph in the right.
place Will . yield a - bund-ant fruit - age, True right -eous-ness and grace.

My re - ward is ev - er with me, For the law of growth is
Then let me lay up treas - ure Be - yond the lapse of

sure; Ev - er sow - ing to the spir - it Will e - ter - nal life se - cure.
time, In that home of heav'n-ly beau - ty Which will be for - ev - er mine.

222

Jordan.

"Come unto me, all ye that labor and are heavy laden, and I will give you rest."—Matt. xi: 28.

Canterbury, N. H.

What saith the Spir - it to the poor and oppressed? "Come un - to me and I will give you rest." Are ye heav-y la - den? have ye fall-en by the way? Jor - dan hath the pow'r of heal - ing. Brave ye the bil - lows now and a - gain, Heal - ing from blind - ness, from sor - row and pain. O be per - suad-ed the wa-ters to try, God in His mer - cy is deal - ing.

Immortal Treasure.

"Well done, thou good and faithful servant: enter thou into the joy of thy lord."— Matt. xxv: 21.

Canterbury, N. H.

Sing, sing, my soul, of that im - mor - tal treas-ure, The bless - ing re-served as the

vic - tor's re-ward; Wrought by de - ni - al of all that of - fend -eth, In

life or in pur-pose, the spir - it of God. Sweet - er by far than the

plaud-its of mil - lions Gained in the con - flict for fame and re - nown, Shall

be the re-turn: "Well done, faithful ser-vant," Sure-ly My love is thy joy and thy crown.

Message.

"All things whatsoever ye would that men should do unto you, do ye even so to them." — Matt. vii : 12.

Canterbury, N. H.

1. There comes down the a - ges a mes - sage of love, Through our
2. O mes - sage so sa - cred, so might - y thy pow'r ! Tho' the

Sav - iour its mer - cies we know :"What - so - ev - er ye would that men do un - to
con - flicts of life may a - bide, Where - so - ev - er thy law finds rest in the

you, Un - to them shall ye do e - ven so." Would ye at the fountain drink
soul Comes the love of the Christ as a guide. Teach us of thy ho - ly,

life ev - er new ?Would ye swell the glad tid - ings of peace, peace, peace ?
bless - ed con - trol ; As in heav'n bring to earth hallowed peace, peace, peace ;

Then call thou thy neigh - bor, thy broth - er, there - to, In their
Thy sway holds the Christ as a pow'r in the soul, Bid - ding

Message.

bless - ing thine own, Thine own, shall in-crease, thine own shall in-crease.
wind and wave, Earth's tur-moil, to cease, earth's tur - moil to cease.

God's Favor.

" They that wait upon the Lord shall renew their strength." — Isa. xl : 31.

Canterbury, N. H.

Wait up - on My time, saith the Lord of hosts, And I will ap-pear un - to

you A pil - lar of fire, and the word of truth Shall dai - ly thy spir - it re - new.

Who shall de - clare that My ar - mor is weak, Or prove that My prom - is - es

fail ? I am ev - er with the hum-ble and meek, And in righteousness they pre - vail.

Higher.

"Here am I, for thou didst call me." — 1 Sam. iii: 6.

Canterbury, N. H.

1. An-gels call me, call me high-er To a realm of pur-er thought; Call me
2. Ev-er call-ing are the an-gels, Call-ing to the heights di-vine, Call-ing

to the foun-tain nigh-er Where the gems of truth are wrought.
where the gifts im-mor-tal Seek my spir-it to re-fine.

Call me here to love and wor-ship, Here to serve and learn God's
All of life it is to serve them, All of joy to find their

way. Rise, my soul, re-newed, re-spon-sive, Meet the Christ that calls to-day.
pow'r; Rise, my soul, thy friend-ship deep-en With the Christ that calls each hour.

Light of Lights.

"Arise, shine ; for thy light is come, and the glory of the Lord is risen upon thee." — Isa. lx: 1.

Canterbury, N. H.

1. Light of Lights, beam on my way, Bear - ing more of truth each day ;
2. Light of Lights, Thy rays di - vine Cheer the way, my heart re - fine,

Shin - ing thro' the realm of thought, E - ter - nal life re - veal - ing.
Strength'ning con-science as they shine, The high - er joy un - fold - ing.

What a Fa- ther's wis - dom loves, What a Moth-er's care ap-proves,
Ho - ly beams, thy ra -diance lend, Be my help - er, guide, be-friend,

Teach me, for my soul would move With - in Thy bright-ness ev - er.
Teach me, for my soul would bend To heav- en's re - sist - less mold-ing.

Committal.

" My people shall be satisfied with my goodness."— Jer. xxxi : 14.

Canterbury, N. H.

1. My heart to Thy work is com-mit-ted, My hands in Thy ser-vice find
2. A psalm of thanks-giv-ing I ren-der, With bless-ings my cup run-neth

rest; Thy laws to my needs are well fit-ted,— How
o'er; For boun-ties and mer-cies so ten - der My

great-ly my spir-it is blest! O glo - ri - ous, glo - ri - ous foun-
spir-it shall hun-ger no more. O glo - ri - ous, glo - ri - ous sal-

there - on, ...
than gold, ...

da - tion! Most safe - ly I'm build-ing, I'm build-ing there - on, Come
va - tion! Thy treas-ures are rich - er, are rich - er than gold, May

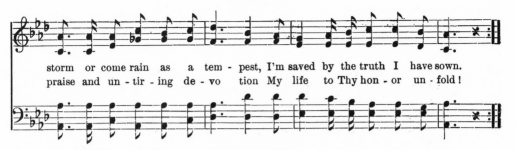

storm or come rain as a tem - pest, I'm saved by the truth I have sown.
praise and un - tir - ing de - vo tion My life to Thy hon - or un - fold !

Bountiful.

"They shall hunger no more, neither thirst any more ; neither shall the sun light on them, nor any
heat." — Rev. vii : 16.

Canterbury, N. H.

O let us not hun - ger nor thirst, The fruits of the spir - it a - bound ; The

rich - es of im - mor - tal truth I'm reap - ing on hal - low - ed ground.

My gos - pel com - pan - ions, we'll rise, Re - joice in the light of to - day ; We

see, as nev - er be - fore, How God doth His mer - cy dis - play.

City of Light.

"Let your light so shine before men, that they may see your good works, and glorify your Father which is in heaven."— Matt. v : 16.

Canterbury, N. H.

1. Lo! ye are the light of the world, A cit-y that can-not be hid; My
2. Lo! ye are dis-ci-ples of mine, My mes-sage so ho-ly pro-claim; In

law, on thy ban-ner un-furled, Shall in ev-'ry king-dom be read.
hon-or and maj-'es-ty shine, That na-tions shall learn of My name.

"So let your light shine be-fore men," That they see your good works and proclaim, The
With cour-age un-daunt-ed and true, Hold a-loft that the wan-d'ring may see, Thy

Lord in His tem-ple is come, His Church is a praise to His name.
bea-con of glo-ry in view, Shall draw need-y souls un-to Me.

Cup of Blessing.

"Whosoever shall give to drink a cup of cold water only in the name of a disciple, he shall in no wise lose his reward." — Matt. x : 42.

Canterbury, N. H.

1. Let me bear the cup of bless-ing As I'm pass-ing to and fro, To the need-y give re-fresh-ing, Love and mer-cy free-ly sow.
2. O the full-ness of this bless-ing! Let me pass it in Christ's name, In the glo-ry of His mis-sion True dis-ci-ple-ship at-tain.

Then I shall be re-mem-bered In the bond of gos-pel care, In the giv-ing and re-ceiv-ing O 'tis joy and peace to share.

Let me share this price-less bless-ing, Let my life re-spond in pray'r, For in hum-ble Chris-tian giv-ing, Bless-ed joy and peace I share.

232

Thy Kingdom Come.

"Thy kingdom come. Thy will be done in earth, as it is in heaven."—Matt. vi: 10.

Canterbury, N. H.

May Thy king - dom come and Thy law be es - tab - lished In the

hearts of Thy peo - ple who dwell here be - low! Thou who rul - est the wind and the

wave at Thy pleas - ure, Wilt Thou hear our pe - ti - tion? Lord, grant it be so.

Do Thou stretch forth Thine arm and shel - ter Thy peo - ple; All the

faith - ful im - plore Thee, the wandering draw near, O re - fresh with Thy ten - der for -

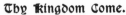

give - ness, the err - ing, Thou, Lord, art our Fa - ther, in mer - cy ap -pear.

Safety.

"And he arose, and rebuked the wind, and said unto the sea, Peace, be still."—Mark iv : 39.

Canterbury, N. H.

We are out on the o - cean broad, Doubts op - press as bil - lows

roar; But our Cap - tain fears no tem - pest, Truth and love His might -y

oar. Nev - er storm that He could not quell, Nev - er lost who hath o -

beyed; They are saved who do His will, On His lov - ing care are stayed.

Forever.

"I will sing of the mercies of the Lord forever." — Psa. lxxxix: 1.

Canterbury, N. H.

No oth-er God will I a-dore For I have felt Je-ho-vah's pow'r, It

called me in a need-y hour To praise His name for-ev-er.

For-ev-er, for-ev-er, For-ev-er and for-ev-er, I'll

give the best, a meas-ure full, A cheer-ful heart, a liv-ing soul, And

through His love I'll be made whole For-ev-er and for-ev-er.

Entreaty.

"He shall give his angels charge concerning thee."— Matt. iv : 6.

Canterbury, N. H.

1. Lead me, lead me, an - gels, lead me To the fount - ain nev - er dry;
2. Guide me, guide me, an - gels, guide me In the path - way of the just;
3. An - gels wait on thy en - treat - y, Sweet re - spons - es greet thy heart;

Heed me, heed me, an - gels, heed me, Do my thirst - y soul sup - ply.
Chide me, chide me, an - gels, chide me, Lest I fal - ter in my trust.
We will kind - ly act our mis - sion, Teach thee of the bet - ter part.

Teach me du - ty, teach me beau - ty In the new and liv - ing way;
Give me ev - er wise en - deav - or, Gos - pel light and truth to sow;
Wis - dom's val - ley is the sur - est, Saf - est ref - uge from the storm,

To the sur - est and the pur - est, I would give my life a - way.
To the bright - est and the whit - est I would heart and hand be - stow.
And her fount - ains are the pur - est,— Make it thy a - bid - ing home.

Harvest Hymn.

"While the earth remaineth, seedtime and harvest shall not cease."— Gen. viii : 22.

Canterbury, N. II.

1. Let our hymn of true thanks-giv - ing Rise in vol - ume sweet and
2. While we rec - og - nize these fa - vors, Let each lov - ing soul ex -

clear, For the bless - ings so a - bun - dant Crown-ing each suc - ceed - ing
pand In - to thought - ful prayer for oth - ers, Not so blest on sea and

year. Blest in reap - ing as in sow - ing, Blest in har - vests gath - ered
land. All are chil - dren of one Fa - ther, In whose u - ni - ver - sal

in, May the earth - ly be a sym - bol Of the fruits of grace we win.
creed We be - hold His boun - ties cov - er E'en the spar - row's dai - ly need.

Ris - ing high - er, strong-er, clear - er, Let our tones of glad - ness
Ris - ing high - er, strong-er, clear - er, Let our tones of glad - ness

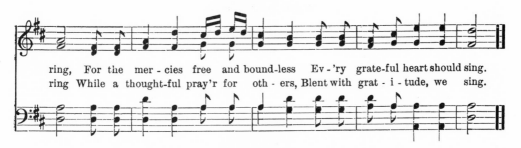

ring, For the mer - cies free and bound-less Ev - 'ry grate-ful heart should sing.
ring While a thought-ful pray'r for oth - ers, Blent with grat - i - tude, we sing.

Anchored.

"And the rain descended, and the floods came, and the winds blew, and beat upon that house; and it fell not: for it was founded upon a rock." — Matt. vii: 25.

Canterbury, N. H.

When the rains de - scend, and the winds shall beat A - gainst the house so

frail, What joy if I may find my feet Well an - chored in the vale

The rock of truth will stand all test, — O let me build there - on, And

with its rev - e - la - tions blest, Foun - da - tion sure is mine.

The Blessing.

"The God of our fathers hath chosen thee, that thou shouldest know his will, and be his witness unto all men."— Acts xxii : 14, 15.

Canterbury, N. H.

When God, as our Fa-ther, shall call for help-ers de-vot-ed and free, What joy, if His bless-ing shall fall in choice and ac-cept-ance of me! A Sav-iour! to pub-lish the word of mer-cy from God's judgment-seat! Here-in is my mis-sion de-clared, here give me soul stat-ure com-plete.

Help One Another.

"Bear ye one another's burdens, and so fulfill the law of Christ."— Gal. vi : 2.

Canterbury, N. H.

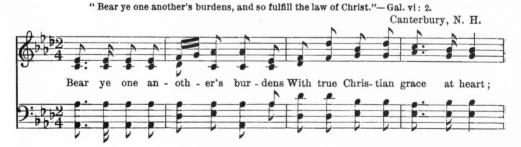

Bear ye one an-oth-er's bur-dens With true Chris-tian grace at heart;

To the doubt-ing give new cour-age, To the wea-ry strength im-part.

O, if faith-ful in your mis-sion, Rich-est bless-ings you shall win;

Yours to gain e-ter-nal heav-en, Ho-li-ness and peace with-in.

Canterbury, N. H.

There's a light that shines on my path-way, A glo-ry in my soul; A

star of hope that bears me on, On to the heav-en-ly goal.

Though clouds a-bove may gath-er, And fear-ful tem-pests rage a-broad;

Yet in my soul is per-fect rest, A treas-ure sent of God.

Consolation.

"Could ye not watch with me one hour?" — Matt. xxvi: 40.

Sabbathday Lake, Me.

1. Watch-ing and pray-ing I find you, O my be-lov-ed, my
2. Watch-ing and pray-ing, the bless-ing Shall for all bur-den a-

own, Trust-ing a Fa-ther's rich prom-ise, I will not leave you a-lone,
tone, Crown-ing your vig-ils so pa-tient, I will not leave you a-lone,

I will not leave you a-lone. Tho' thro' the des-ert I lead, Or a-
I will not leave you a-lone. When trib-u-la-tions op-press, When re-

part in the moun-tain ye pray For strength in the hour of need, I
vers-es en-dan-ger the way, Heav'n's host shall encompass and bless; I

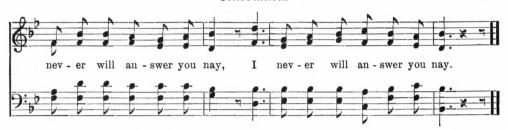

nev - er will an - swer you nay, I nev - er will an - swer you nay.

Justice.

"Let all those that put their trust in thee rejoice: let them ever shout for joy."—Psa. v : 11.

Enfield, N. H.

O Lord, in Thee I place my trust As mor - tal strength doth fail ; I know that jus - tice, love and truth, Will fi - nal - ly pre - vail. The clouds that may ob - scure the sight, Ere long will pass a - way, As real - ly as the dark - est night Pre - cedes the dawn - ing day

Service of Love.

"God hath not given us the spirit of fear ; but of power, and of love."—2 Tim. i: 7.

Canterbury, N. H.

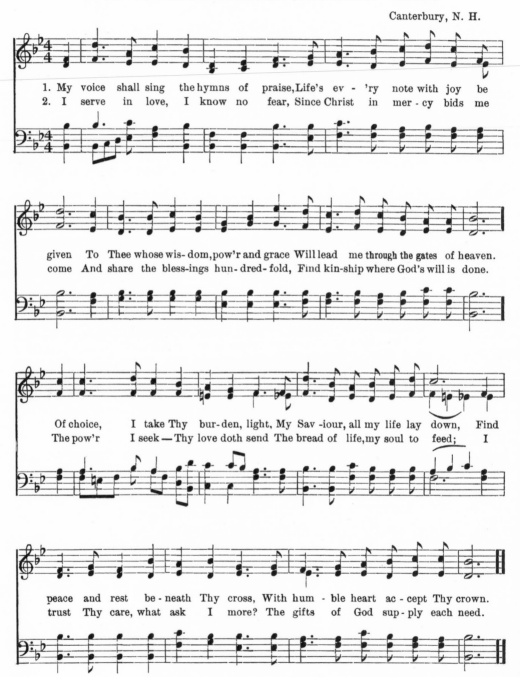

1. My voice shall sing the hymns of praise, Life's ev - 'ry note with joy be
2. I serve in love, I know no fear, Since Christ in mer - cy bids me

given To Thee whose wis- dom, pow'r and grace Will lead me through the gates of heaven.
come And share the bless-ings hun- dred- fold, Find kin-ship where God's will is done.

Of choice, I take Thy bur- den, light, My Sav -iour, all my life lay down, Find
The pow'r I seek — Thy love doth send The bread of life, my soul to feed; I

peace and rest be - neath Thy cross, With hum - ble heart ac - cept Thy crown.
trust Thy care, what ask I more? The gifts of God sup - ply each need.

Press On.

" Press toward the mark for the prize of the high calling of God."— Phil. iii: 14.

Canterbury, N. H.

1. Press on, on tri-umph-ant-ly, The vic-to-ry is sure to come; Tho'
2. Press on, on, tho' fears as-sail, Tho' rest-less doubts op-press thy soul; For

clouds oft ob-scure the day, Trust in God's al-might-y arm. He'll
God's love shall still pre-vail While e-ter-nal a-ges roll. From

lead thee o'er the mount-ain high, And thro' the bar-ren plains of doubt; Will
threat-'ning foe He bids thee rise To join the hosts of strength so near; His

prove that He is ev-er nigh,—On sure ground He'll bring thee out.
shield of faith will guard the wise, Press on, on, be-yond all fear.

In the Valley.

"Thou art with me; thy rod and thy staff they comfort me."—Psa. xxiii: 4.

Canterbury, N. H.

1. Down in the val-ley where liv-ing wa-ters flow, What
2. Down in the val-ley the keen-est winds pass by, There

joy and sweet peace the soul there may know! O bless me, my Sav-iour, and
tran-quil and brave my spir-it shall lie, The still small voice can reach me with

keep me ev-er low, Down in the val-ley where liv-ing wa-ters flow.
mes-sage from on high, Down in the val-ley where God is ev-er nigh.

There's heal-ing in Jor-dan and power to sus-tain The soul through all tri-als the
There's rest in the val-ley no power can ex-plain, Earth's highlands of hon-or I

truth to main-tain, There's a fount of liv-ing wa-ters from
seek not to gain, I've a cov-ert safe and rest-ful where

In the Valley.

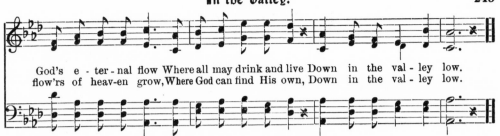

God's e - ter - nal flow Where all may drink and live Down in the val - ley low.
flow'rs of heav-en grow, Where God can find His own, Down in the val - ley low.

Realms of Light.

" Drop down ye heavens from above, and let the skies pour down righteousness.'' — Isa. xlv : 8.

Canterbury, N. H.

Ye heav - ens, realms of ho - ly light, now o - pen wide the por - tals, Our

souls ad - vanc - ing in - to right, sing praise with the im - mor - tals. Ye
While

sta - tioned here for test - ing work, for growth by self - de - ni - al We
oft to an - gel hosts would look for strength thro' earth-ly tri - al. While
Ye

The Soul's Plea.

"I will not let thee go, except thou bless me." — Gen. xxxii : 26.

Canterbury, N. H.

I plead my cause be - fore Thee, Lord, I wres - tle in my prayer For
in - spi - ra - tion from Thy word, For wis - dom, love and care.
O Fa - ther, least a - mong Thy flock, Thou'lt feed me by the way; And
guide me to the liv - ing Rock, Whose wa - ters are my stay.

My Confidence.

"But see ye first the kingdom of God, and his righteousness." — Matt. vi : 33.

Canterbury, N. H.

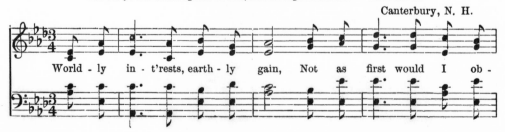

World - ly in - t'rests, earth - ly gain, Not as first would I ob -

tain; Heav-en's king - dom, rich - es there, Have my con - fi - dence and care.

What has helped me hith - er - to Is the love that mak - eth

true; Truth has stayed life's dangerous wave, And in Christ will bind and save.

Canterbury, N. H.

There's a bright, bright sphere of truth and love, O pil-grim, don't de - spair; But

step by step, with a trust - ing heart, Thy cross and bur - den bear.

Lay down thy life, thy self - ish care, And in the broad field la - bor; To

near thy God, be pure at heart, Deal just - ly with thy neigh - bor.

Benediction.

"Lord, lift thou up the light of thy countenance upon us." — Psa. iv: 6.

Canterbury, N. H.

On the work of our hands And the praise of our hearts, May the

light of Thy coun - te - nance shine, ... In the least ev - er
coun - te - nance shine,

faith - ful, a - bid - ing and true, Our serv - ice of joy shall be Thine.

May the ha - lo of pray'r And the man - tle of peace As

heav'n's ben - e - dic - tion de - scend, ... Or - dain - ing our
ben - e - dic - tion de - scend,

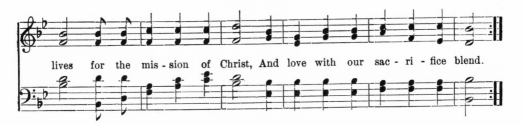

lives for the mis - sion of Christ, And love with our sac - ri - fice blend.

Good Report.

" And I am come to bring you unto a good land, unto a land flowing with milk and honey."—Ex. iii: 8.

Canterbury, N. H.

I have set my heart to jour - ney To the land of good re -

port, Where is flow - ing milk and hon - ey And the wine of heaven - ly fruit.

And I'm trac - ing here my gar - ments Seek - ing truth with peace and

love, For they wear no oth - er rob - ing In those bliss - ful realms a - bove.

Live for God.

"There is no want to them that fear him." — Psalm xxxiv: 9.

Canterbury, N. H.

Who lives for God shall nev - er want, Though in the need - y

hour; For trust - ing in His love di - vine, Will prove sus - tain - ing power.

O may my soul be wise and true, Un - to the end en -

dure; For on - ly to the faith - ful few Christ's promise is se - cure.

At Parting.

"Whither I go ye know and the way ye know."—St. John xiv: 4.

Canterbury, N. H.

1. We'll meet you in the land of souls, With gar - ments white, in -
2. Pass on, brave heart, thy lamp of life Has dimmed to mor - tal

wrought; Rich treas-ures we are stor - ing there, As Christ our Sav - iour taught.
eyes, But o'er the hills of God we see Thy sun of glo - ry rise.

And as ye pass thro' realms of light, At- tained by peace and
Our spir - its chas-tened by the strife With pow'rs of earth - ly

prayer, O turn in lov - ing thought to those Still bound by earth - ly care.
mold, When time and tide shall yield their sway, We'll meet on strands of gold.

Raise the Standard.

"Lift up a standard for the people." — Isa. lxii: 10.

Canterbury, N. H.

1. O lift the stand-ard high-er up, The vir-gin ban-ner wide un-furl, Pro-
2. The nar-row way by Chris-tians taught Is up the rug-ged heights of truth; Then
3. Who-ev-er bears the stand-ard high With pur-pose loy-al to its name, Can

claim-ing life and lib-er-ty In du-al Christ un-to the world. Yea,
lift the stand-ard where you've fought, To mark the way for age and youth. Yea,
ev-'ry prin-ci-ple de-fy, Which would a Chris-tian's hon-or stain. Yea,

lift the stand-ard high-er up, Let truth in re-gal glo-ry reign, Till

na-tions clasp her gold-en cup To drink the power that shall sus-tain.

Our Mission.

"Let us draw near with a true heart, in full assurance of faith."—Heb. x : 22.

Canterbury, N. H.

1. Our Fa - ther, we ask Thee To still be our friend, To
2. We'll cheer - ful - ly serve Thee, And do Thy whole will; On,
3. We ask not for pleas - ure, We seek not for gain, The

lead us still on, For on Thee we de - pend, For com - fort in
grant us Thy wis - dom and pow'r to ful - fill Christ's work of re -
joy of full serv - ice is all that we claim. Our life we will

sor - row, For strength to main - tain The work of our Sav - iour, Thy
demp - tion Now here on the earth, That souls may be sav - ed And
of - fer A liv - ing sac - ri - fice, That God's glo - rious mis - sion On

word has made plain, The work of our Sav - iour Thy word has made plain.
find the new birth, That souls may be sav - ed And find the new birth.
earth be re - vived, That God's glo - rious mis - sion On earth be re - vived.

Sweet Angels.

"Lead me in thy truth, and teach me."— Psa. xxv: 5.

Canterbury, N. H.

1. Sweet an - gels, come near - er, O near - er, and near - er, Do list to our
2. Then near - er, bright an - gels, come near - er, and near - er, Thy in - flu - ence
3. We want our names writ - ten on pa - ges in heav - en, With vows of our

plead-ings for strength from on high; This world's seem - ing pleas - ures, its
ho - ly spread o - ver each heart; In les - sons im - press - ive, hu -
full con - se - cra - tion to God. Be near us, blest an - gels, O

rich - es, its hon -ors, The im - mor - tal spir - it can nev - er sup - ply.
mil - i - ty teach us, True love and for - give - ness to each one im - part.
ev - er be near us, In - spire and guide till we reach that a - bode.

Gratitude.

"Thanks be unto God for his unspeakable gift." — 2 Cor. ix: 15.

Canterbury, N. H.

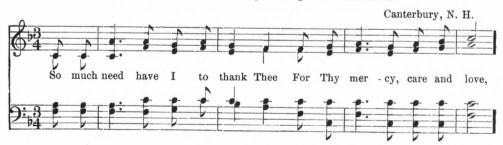

So much need have I to thank Thee For Thy mer - cy, care and love,

That I have no heart to mur-mur, And no lips but to ap-prove.

Teach me how I best may serve Thee, Ev-'ry con-scious hour con-

trol; Then but lit-tle have I giv-en For the wealth that greets my soul.

Canterbury, N. H.

In your prayers re-mem-ber me, Am I not a chos-en

one? I must bear the test a-lone, I must do as ye have done.

Ye who've o-ver-come the world, Ye who stand where I would

dwell, Make your in-ter-ces-sions strong, That with me it may be well.

None Too Much Time.

"So teach us to number our days, that we may apply our hearts unto wisdom." — Psa. xc : 12.

Canterbury, N. H.

1. Time may be long and full length of days giv'n, E - ter - ni - ty prom - is - ing
2. Time may be brief, let us num - ber our days That God may ap-prove, at the

life with - out end ; But "None too much time,"the mes-sen - ger whis-pers,"Tho'
set of life's sun, Our meas - ure of love, as proof of the ser - vice Of

ev - 'ry ex - pres - sion as praise should as - cend." Ah ! none too much time to
heart and of hand, as His will here is done. Ah ! none too much time His

blend thy af - fec - tion With fa-thers and moth-ers, the household of God ; None too much
mes-sage to pub - lish, So ma - ny have need of thy heart's rich-est tone ; None too much

time   to bless all   the chil-dren, For lov -ing and blessing brings hap-py   re - ward.
time — O treas-ure it   wise-ly, For God, at thy hand, is   re - quir -ing His own.

Higher Up.

"Look unto me and be ye saved, all the ends of the earth."—Isa. xlv : 22.

Canterbury, N. H.

Look   a   lit - tle high - er   up, High - er   up,   high - er   up,

Look   a   lit - tle high - er   up,   A voice from heav'n is   call - ing.

High - er   up   for truth and right, High - er   up   for   gos - pel   sight,

High - er where from   wis - dom's height Pure   rays   of   light   are   fall - ing.

My Mission.

"Even as the Son of man came not to be ministered unto, but to minister."—Matt. xx: 28.

Canterbury, N. H.

1. O   what is the mis-sion ap-point-ed to me As the days come and
2. Go   strength-en the fee - ble, en - cour - age the strong; Be   thou as a
3. "And do not your alms to be hon-ored of men,"Was the Sav-iour's in -
4. Like the dil - i - gent cor - al be - neath the deep sea, Toil thou for the

go   and the swift mo-ments flee? It is live to do good whereso-e'er is your
light, a   joy, a new song; Seek on - ly the wis-dom that comes from a -
junc-tion so sim - ple and plain; But give to the need-y, thus lend to the
fu - ture tho' hid -den may be The struct-ure you build by de - vo -tion and

call, And give to the house-hold your serv - ic - es all. Ah, this is the
bove, First ho - ly, then peace-ful, a - bound-ing in love.
Lord For these ye have al - ways and ye have your re - ward.
care, If found-ed in vir - tue its worth will ap - pear.

mis- sion ap-point-ed to me, As the days come and go, and the swift mo-ments flee.

Test of Love.

"If ye love me keep my commandments."—St. John xiv: 15.

Canterbury, N. H.

1. "If ye love Me," comes the message, If ye love My will to do,
2. "If ye love Me!" O the power Vest-ed here Christ's call to heed!

Keep My word, a-bide My coun-sel, That I may a-bide with you.
"More than these" ex-alts the mis-sion Lambs of God with love to feed.

As ye give, will be the meas-ure Of the bless-ing given to thee;
Source di-vine, be ours, tho' hid-den From the pow'rs that test and try!

What-so-ev-er thy pe-ti-tion In My name will grant-ed be.
Naught can foil the will e-ter-nal Where the soul finds heav'n's supply.

Tempest=Tossed.

" I will be glad and rejoice in thy mercy: for thou hast considered my trouble ; thou hast known my soul in adversities."— Psa. xxxi: 7.

Canterbury, N. H.

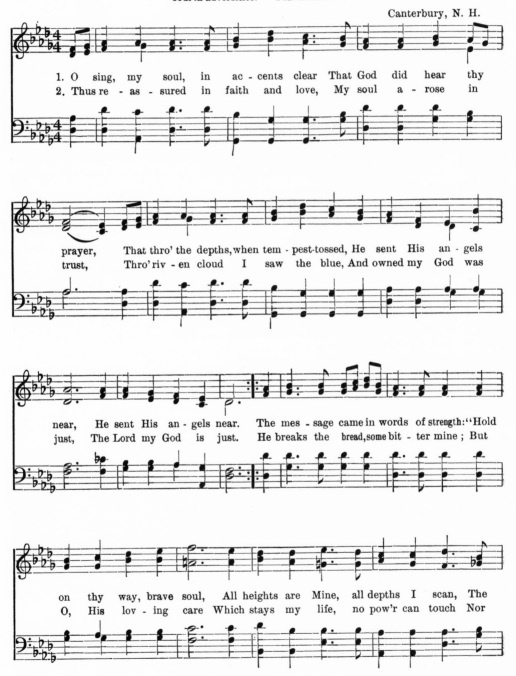

1. O sing, my soul, in ac-cents clear That God did hear thy
2. Thus re - as - sured in faith and love, My soul a - rose in

prayer, That thro' the depths, when tem - pest-tossed, He sent His an - gels
trust, Thro' riv - en cloud I saw the blue, And owned my God was

near, He sent His an - gels near. The mes - sage came in words of strength:"Hold
just, The Lord my God is just. He breaks the bread, some bit - ter mine ; But

on thy way, brave soul, All heights are Mine, all depths I scan, The
O, His lov - ing care Which stays my life, no pow'r can touch Nor

waves will I con - trol, The waves will I con - trol."
with its force com - pare, Nor with its force com - pare.

Heirs of Salvation.

"Heirs of God and joint-heirs with Christ." — Rom. viii : 17.

Canterbury, N. H.

Who shall reach the heights of glo - ry, Find as - cent by faith and

prayer, Save the soul whose life is ho - ly, Heir to God's e - ter - nal care.

Such are crowned with self - de - ni - al, Walk the new and liv - ing

way, Step by step through earthly tri - al To the wealth of end - less day.

True Riches.

"For wnat shall it profit a man, if he shall gain the whole world, and lose his own soul?" — Mark viii : 36.

Canterbury, N. H.

1. Be fixed, my heart, on high - er aims Than seek - ing world - ly
2. En - list my thought on no - bler themes Than fame or wealth in -
3. Let pur - er mo - tives guide my feet In wis - dom's ways so
4. What prof - it, e'en to gain a world Of E - den joys or

pleas - ure ; Thy long-ing spir - it hath its claims On an e - ter - nal treas - ure.
spires, For these shall pass like i - dle dreams Be-fore truth's al - tar fires.
pleas - ant, Since fut - ure bliss is made complete By guard-ing well the pres-ent.
glo - ry, If by our gain we lose the soul In depths of sin and fol - ly ?

Ah ! – " What shall it profit a man, if he gain the whole world, and lose his own soul ?"

Triumph.

"Be of good cheer ; I have overcome the world." — St. John xvi : 33.

Canterbury, N. H.

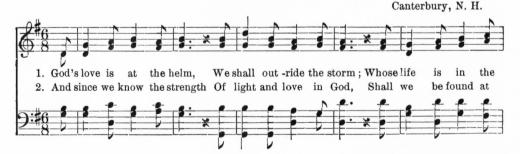

1. God's love is at the helm, We shall out -ride the storm ; Whose life is in the
2. And since we know the strength Of light and love in God, Shall we be found at

light   Can fear   no earth - ly harm.   The pas - sage may   be   long   Ere
length   As those who doubt His word?   Nay, truth our path   shall   fill   And

truth o'er er - ror rise,   But they are al - ways strong Who make no com-pro -mise.
bring a cloud-less sky;   We'll trust and do His will   And all   our foes de - fy.

Enfield, N. H.

I will go   on my way, and I   will   not look back, My march is   for

Heav - en, that beau - ti - ful land, Where ros - es and lil - ies e -

ter - nal - ly bloom, And sor - row and sigh - ing shall nev - er - more come.

My faith is es - tab - lished, the road it is sure, My call - ing is

sa - cred, and   I will en - dure   All cross - es   and tri - als that

come in my way;   I will con - quer and reign, in this beau - ti - ful day.

Comforted.

"I will make an everlasting covenant with you, even the sure mercies of David." — Isa. lv: 3.

Canterbury, N. H.

In the day when I shall com - fort thee, what shall be thy re - joic - ing,

If thy cov - e - nant with Me is found un - bro - ken, O Zi - on!

I will lift up thy head a - bove all thy af - flic - tion, And My

most glo - ri - ous prom - is - es shall be in thee ful - filled.

Christ's Promise.

"The blind receive their sight, and the lame walk, the lepers are cleansed, and the deaf hear, ＊ ＊ and the poor have the gospel preached to them." — Matt. xi: 5.

Canterbury, N. H.

The blind shall see, the deaf shall hear, The lame re-stored shall be, The lep - er cleansed, the

err -ing sav'd, Who come, saith Christ, to Me. "My king - dom is not of this world," My

serv -ants can not fight; But to re - deem, cre-ate a - new, I came on earth with light.

Encouragement.

"As thy days, so shall thy strength be." — Deut. xxxiii : 25.

Canterbury, N. H.

Let no one be dis-heart-ened, Nor count the vict'ries small, God's love is ev - er

watch - ful, And knows thy ef - forts all. And as thy day, most sure-ly Thy

light and strength shall be; As drops that fill the o - cean, So gains will come to thee.

God's Blessing.

"I will lift up mine eyes unto the hills, from whence cometh my help."—Psa. cxxi: 1.

Canterbury, N. H.

1. As the dawn of the morn-ing, Or a heav-en-ly ray, God's
2. As the breath of the morn-ing, As the strength of the hills, God's
3. As the dew of the morn-ing, Or as bright riv-ers roll, So

glo - ri - ous brightness Il - lu -mines my way. I will sing of His fa - vor, Would
bless-ing re - stor-eth, My meas-ure re - fills. His will as my sunshine, My
free - ly God's blessings Flow in - to my soul. I will walk in His pres-ence As

mer - it His love, By hon - est en - deav -or My loy - al - ty prove.
dai - ly em - ploy, No mur - mur of sad -ness Can cloud or an - noy.
one great - ly blest, On whose soul the love of His work is im-pressed.

Building.

"We have a building of God, an house not made with hands, eternal in the heavens.—2 Cor. v: 1.

Canterbury, N. H.

1. O build-er, would'st thou raise A house not made with hands, A mon - u -ment of
2. Let ev - 'ry voice be stilled Save one which sings a - new, O build thou, wise-ly

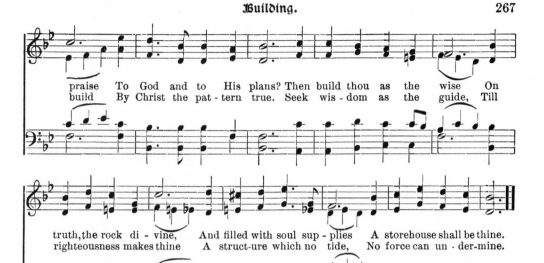

praise To God and to His plans? Then build thou as the wise On
build By Christ the pat-tern true. Seek wis-dom as the guide, Till

truth, the rock di - vine, And filled with soul sup - plies A storehouse shall be thine.
righteousness makes thine A struct-ure which no tide, No force can un - der-mine.

Self=Denial.

" God forbid that I should glory, save in the cross of Christ."— Gal. vi: 14.

Canterbury, N. H.

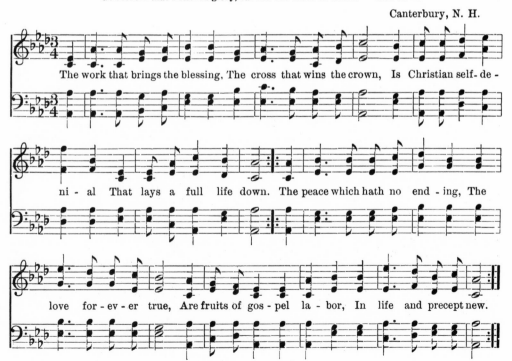

The work that brings the blessing, The cross that wins the crown, Is Christian self- de -

ni - al That lays a full life down. The peace which hath no end - ing, The

love for - ev - er true, Are fruits of gos - pel la - bor, In life and precept new.

Silver Lining.

"The fruit of the Spirit is love, joy, peace."—Gal. v: 22.

Canterbury, N. H.

1. Joy and peace are my sun-shine, And no day so o - ver-
2. In God's love is my ref - uge, So the day is ev - er

cast, But I catch the sil - ver lin - ing, Shin-ing thro' the storm-y blast;
bright, For I share His kind pro - tec - tion, And I fear no dark-some night.

Shin - ing thro' a par - ent's bless - ing, Thro' a love and coun - sel
In the tu - mult 'mid life's bat - tle I can hear God's un - der-

pure, Lead - ing on from earth - ly fail - ure To a home and heav'n se - cure.
tone; With His peace my soul is light - ed, And His mer - cies rich I own.

Tarry Not.

"Seek those things which are above." —Col. iii: 1.

Canterbury, N. H.

1. O tar-ry not 'mid world-ly strife, But press for high-er gain;
2. O tar-ry not 'mid world-ly strife, But seek the gifts a-bove;

Christ taught the pure, the per-fect life, Where right-eous-ness shall reign.
Pow'r di-vine to guide the life, True wis-dom, light and love.

There's no dis-cord-ant mu-sic where Sweet peace and love con-trol;
These high-er truths at-tract my heart, Where wealth of soul is giv'n,

Joy and wor-ship, praise and pray'r, Rise as in-cense from the soul.
Bid me choose with Christ a part, My cross, my crown, my heav'n.

Response.

"Shall the dust praise thee? shall it declare thy truth? Thou hast girded me with gladness; to the end that my glory may sing praise to thee, and not be silent."— Psa. xxx : 9–12.

Canterbury, N. H.

1. Shall earth re - spond with har - vest full To God's great love and
2. Bring forth thy vows in grate - ful prayer, And sound thy prais - es

care, And thou be si - lent, O my soul, For gifts thou'rt blest to share?
high; The Lord hath dealt thee rich - est grace, His gifts are ev - er nigh.

A - wake to new - ness ev - 'ry hour, To high - er aims and true, And
Re - spon - sive rise in ho - lier tho't, In ma - jes - ty of peace, And

seek by right - eous - ness that power Which crowns the faith - ful few.
let thy life full trib - ute sing As ben - e - fits in - crease.

Index

(Anthems indicated by *)

271